Memoir of the Sunday Brunch

Center Point
Large Print

**This Large Print Book carries the
Seal of Approval of N.A.V.H.**

Memoir of the Sunday Brunch

Julia Pandl

CENTER POINT LARGE PRINT
THORNDIKE, MAINE

This Center Point Large Print edition
is published in the year 2013 by arrangement with
Algonquin Books of Chapel Hill,
a divison of Workman Publishing.

The text of this Large Print edition is unabridged.
In other aspects, this book may vary
from the original edition.
Printed in the United States of America
on permanent paper.
Set in 16-point Times New Roman type.

ISBN: 978-1-61173-648-9

Library of Congress Cataloging-in-Publication Data

Pandl, Julia, 1970–
 Memoir of the Sunday brunch / Julia Pandl. — Center Point large print
edition.
 pages cm
 ISBN 978-1-61173-648-9 (library binding : large print : alk. paper)
 1. Pandl, Julia, 1970– 2. Pandl, George.
  3. Restaurateurs—United States—Biography.
  4. Authors—United States—Biography.
  5. Restaurants—Wisconsin—Milwaukee—Biography.
  6. Fathers and daughters. 7. Large type books. I. Title.
TX950.5.P36A3 2013
647.95092—dc23
[B]
                                                        2012040121

To my parents,
George and Terry,
for showing me the way.

And to my siblings,
Johnny, Jimmy, Katie, Peggy, Chrissy, Amy,
Stevie, and Jeremiah,
for showing me a whole bunch of other stuff.

And to everyone whose first job
was at George Pandl's in Bayside.

Contents

Author's Note

·————

These are my stories as I remember them—the ones that have survived the march of time and left their mark. Granted, my memory is not what it used to be, but I tried to be as true to the events as possible. One or two names have been omitted or changed to protect the innocent, the guilty, and the disgusting.

PART I

All the world's a stage,
And all the men and women merely players;
They have their exits and their entrances;
And one man in his time plays many parts . . .

—William Shakespeare, *As You Like It*

1

Blueberry or Plain

I thought my dad was just like every other dad, until the day I worked my first Sunday brunch. I stepped over a line that afternoon, a thin wrinkle in time, hanging in the ether between breakfast and lunch. It was subtle, a wisp of a moment, like God giggling as he licked his thumb and turned the page on Providence. Distracted by the fact that my father had traded his sanity for a paper chef hat and a set of utility tongs, I missed it— but the moment happened. They say the Lord rested on the seventh day. Not so. He went out to brunch with the rest of creation.

I began working at my father's restaurant, with the rest of my siblings, at twelve. George, my father, enlisted all of us at an early age. Child labor laws didn't apply back then in our family, so my father could do anything he wanted with us, and he did. There were nine of us: Johnny, Jimmy, Katie, Peggy, Chrissy, Amy, Steve, Jeremiah, and me. I never thought there was anything unusually large about my family. I still don't. Today, when people hear nine kids, they always gasp. The gasp that offers an implied "a lot" or "too many" or "holy cow." But when you're number nine, when you're the last one who arrives at the party, just before time runs out and the uterine door is slammed shut forever, you don't gasp—you sigh. I suppose some of the older siblings, the ones forced to rinse out poopy diapers left soaking in the toilet before they used it, may have occasionally thought eight or nine was one or two too many, but not me. I never saw what life looked like without them. Sure, I imagined it, every time Jeremiah stuck his disgusting bulbous white wart in my face, but that just doesn't count. To me, nine was normal.

I never saw what life looked like before the restaurant either. It was present in the definition of our family—the member that equaled the whole. Employment there, when we were kids, was simply understood. Every day the sun came up, and food needed to be prepared. I never heard a single conversation regarding whether or not one of my siblings would go to work. What I *did* hear was the phone ringing, someone calling in sick, and Peggy and Chrissy fighting about whose turn it was to go. Perhaps we could have unionized, but we were too scared, and too small, to think of such a thing. The eight of them went before me, some before their tenth birthday, so I guess I was lucky.

Here's how I ended up in my father's chain gang: I slipped up and got caught stealing time on the sofa.

It was July, I think, 1982. Our summer cottage in Cedar Grove had become our permanent residence the previous August. It was a Swiss chalet replica tucked at the end of a gravel road along the Wisconsin shore of Lake Michigan. I had access to some of the most pristine beach in North America, yet instead I chose to watch TV. Late one beautiful Saturday morning, George, my father, caught me lying on our woolly plaid couch, still in my Lanz nightgown, watching *The Lone Ranger*. That was the moment I kissed unemployment good-bye.

Admittedly, it was a rookie mistake. Even at twelve, I knew enough to run from the TV when I heard his footsteps on the loose floorboard outside their bedroom door. Television existed in our house for the moon landing, assassinations, and my mother's sanity. Period. For us kids, any enjoyment via TV was strictly prohibited.

So that morning, my father went on a semi-hysterical tirade about a beautiful summer day, reading a book, laziness, and the covered-wagon days.

I just sat there with my mouth open.

Then, his parting words, "You're coming with me to work the brunch tomorrow," slapped me out of the television's tranquil grip.

Maybe I sabotaged myself, because in truth, I was actually excited to go. I adored my siblings, and aside from Jeremiah, they had been trickling out the door, one by one, for years. Johnny and Jimmy were married with families of their own, and the rest were either in college or getting ready to start. When they did come home on weekends and holidays, usually to work, I felt an excitement that I think is unique to the babies of the family—and puppies. If I'd had a tail, it would have wagged. So I raced to catch up with them; anything they were allowed to do that I wasn't held a delicious mystique. Once in a while, as our parents slept, my siblings secretly let me sit on a lap at the kitchen table in my pajamas, teaching me how to fold pizza and say "shit" while they chatted with their friends. But their time at the restaurant had still remained a mystery. After a full day at work, they came home with hands smelling of smoked fish and stale strawberries. I heard tales of needle-nose pliers and slipping the pinbones from a side of whitefish. They never talked much about George. Looking back, it seems a little odd. I honestly don't think it ever occurred to any of them to alert me, to say something like, "Hey, head's up, Dad's . . . um . . . not quite right on Sundays, so don't do anything stupid." That would have been nice, but it's not how they rolled. In a family business, some things, no matter how out of the ordinary, are just accepted as "normal." They didn't know any better; there-fore, neither did I. All I knew was that when my time finally came, I would clean flat after flat of strawberries. And I would do it as well and as quickly as my siblings did, if not better and faster.

OF COURSE, I had been at the restaurant hundreds of times. More often than not, though, I was just along for the ride. I had never worked an entire day. Sometimes I carried a five-gallon pickle bucket and cleaned the parking lot of candy wrappers and chewed gum, but mostly I just sat at the bar, ate hot fudge sundaes, and waited for someone to take me home. My sister Katie would make fluffy grasshoppers for the customers, then pour me the remains from the blender. It was wickedly cool, minty, and grown up.

My father didn't wear a suit, sit at a desk, or hang around a water cooler, but his job at the restaurant seemed regular enough to me. I never gave it much thought. Truth be told, I didn't really care. He left the house early every day and he came home late. He brought home raw meat and other unidentifiable leftovers from his office. So what? Aside from that, George was just like every other dad: he dressed like a goober and was never home. Saturday mornings were when we usually saw him. Before going to work, he made us eggs, any way we liked them: scrambled, fried, over easy, over hard, stomped on, or perfectly soft-boiled.

On the rare night he was home, my father read to me: *Stuart Little*, *Little Women*, *Little House on the Prairie*. Lots of Littles. Before we moved to Cedar Grove, we lived in a redbrick colonial on Prospect Avenue in Milwaukee, a street lined with elm trees and loaded with kids. There were the Hoys, the Reillys, the Popaliskys, the Dineens, the Kliemans, the Kublys, and the O'Laughlins, and each family had a pile of kids. There was chaos everywhere, tumbling in every dryer, left in every driveway, smoking behind every garage, and stuck to the bottom of every shoe. One family on the block, the Downeys, had only two kids. The father was a world-renowned composer, the mother a famous opera singer. Their son and daughter channeled their energy into creative pursuits such as piano playing and ballet dancing. The rest of us channeled our energy into fashioning bongs out of soda cans and lighting stuff on fire.

Our house had six proper bedrooms; the seventh, a converted walk-in closet, was mine. I was an "oops" baby. I slept in a youth bed—not quite a twin but not a crib either—shoved up against the wall. When George came in to visit me, he had to squeeze in like a sardine in a can, head on the pillow, feet on the top of the footboard. I liked to sandwich between him and the wall, folding myself in half, resting my head on his big belly, with my dirty feet up on the wall and my knees around my ears. My room was a comfy spot. During those visits, I sucked my thumb and listened to my dad's soft voice reading about Stuart Little's adventures. Every now and then I caught him reading with his eyes closed. His ability to see the words through the puffy, pinkish folds of his eyelids was downright supernatural. I guess after eight kids he didn't need the book anymore; he could just recite the story by heart. Still, it scared the bejesus out of me.

Like most dads, he had various and exceptionally irritating ways of waking us up. Some mornings, he'd enter our rooms wearing only his boxers, slapping his stomach as if it were a snare drum and singing, "School days, school days, good ole golden rule days." Other days he whipped open the shades and bellowed, "Rise and shine, daylight in the swamps!" The *most* offensive was the Bee. He entered buzzing, pulled off the covers, and pinched us repeatedly, until irritation finally got us out of bed. Glasses of cold water were used on my dope-smoking siblings.

My father did not golf or play tennis. He did not run, swim, or jog. Once in a while, before we moved to Cedar Grove, he'd ride his bike to work. He wore a white button-down oxford shirt, red tartan plaid pants secured tightly around his right ankle with a rubber band, black socks, and brown wingtip shoes. His stomach was rock hard and rounded, like a watermelon, his legs skinny, like bamboo shoots with feet. He kept in shape by drinking beer and brandy Manhattans—not at the same time—and eating cheese so noxious it could be melted and used to strip varnish. He kept his hair cut tennis-ball short. He never napped. He wore bow ties decorated with unicorns, which, on him, were never stuffy. They just said: "Damn glad to meet you."

ON MY FIRST Sunday brunch, we pulled into the parking lot a little before eight in the morning, my eyes still swollen with sleep. George looked at me and said, "Wait here."

What's this? I thought. *He's not even going to let me out of the car.*

He returned a few minutes later, knocked on the window, and held up the pickle bucket. "Pick up the parking lot," he said.

Outside, I was immediately covered in a blanket of July heat. The humidity filled my lungs like a sack of wet gym socks.

"It's gonna be a scorcher today," he said, chuckling as he walked in the restaurant's back door.

Picking up the parking lot was among the dirtier jobs at the restaurant, but nothing compared to cleaning out the grease trap. It looked pretty harmless to me, but according to my siblings, opening it released olfactory horrors that could cause brain damage. If you complained about another job, George often threatened you with the grease trap, so now I silently took the bucket and headed straight for a pile of cigarette butts. Customers often emptied entire ashtrays right next to their cars with no regard for the small hands that had to pick up the mess. They never put any money in their ashtrays either—just old candy, gum, and aluminum flip tops. I used my bare hands—it never occurred to me that a broom and a dustpan might have been helpful, or even a pair of gloves. The work was delicate and disgusting but better than brain damage.

After I was sufficiently drenched in sweat, George opened the back door and let me in. Finally, I had officially been signed to the team, the ninth man. I stepped across the threshold into my future, the big leagues, the bowels of the basement, where my father would teach me the secret handshake.

He was already dressed: a white chef's T-shirt with snaps, houndstooth check chef's pants rolled up to his shins, and brown socks and shoes covered with what looked like pancake batter, but I knew it was Ammens powder. He had a thing about Ammens. In a constant battle against chafing, he had Fitzgerald's Pharmacy deliver cases of the stuff to the restaurant and the house. Keeping his business dry was a top priority. Of course, chef pants are loose, and so are boxers, so 90 percent of the powder ended up on the carpeting next to his dresser and in the seams of his work shoes.

That Sunday morning I sensed something different about him as he ordered me up the stairs to the kitchen, a tone I didn't recognize. A little pang of dread sprouted in my gut—I'd felt it before, when my brother Jimmy threatened to hang me on the bathroom doorknob by my underpants—but then I smelled the brunch.

Brunch was the best smell in the world. It was real food, *fresh* food, a potpourri of bacon, sausage, strawberries, raspberries, fresh-squeezed orange juice, cookies, cakes, cinnamon buns, and apple strudel, one scent after another, dancing like Fred and Ginger at the party in my nose. I knew then that heaven smelled like Sunday mornings.

After I washed my hands until they were raw, my sister Amy handed me an apron. I was too short to reach the stainless countertop, so she told me to flip my bucket over and hop up. The party ended quickly when she set another bucket next to me, this one filled with cooked shrimp, and said, "Start peeling."

I looked over at a pile of ice full of caraway seeds and celery bottoms. The hot shrimp underneath gave rise to a hot steam that reeked of the sea. The smell made me gag.

"How many should I do?"

"All of 'em."

Crying was not an option, so I laughed. "Seriously?"

"Yeah, c'mon, there's four more buckets over there." She pointed to a spot next to the stove. "Hurry up. We open the doors in an hour and a half. I'll go find you some chef clothes. You're doing pancakes."

I burrowed my fist into the ice. "I can't . . . get—"

"Just do it. Dad's freaking out." She scurried away.

I was going to say, "I can't get at them because my hand is already frozen," but somehow I knew it didn't matter. Instinct kicked in; my hand could freeze solid and fall off, yet brunch would still go on. Judging by the amount of shrimp waiting, that bucket was my destiny.

She did say "chef clothes," though. That was something. Every team member has to have a uniform. I fantasized about looking all cheflike and professional—pants, coat, and tall paper hat like George, maybe even a scarf tied just so around my neck. Amy had said "doing pancakes" too. I had no idea what that meant, but if it was in uniform, I could perform. I'd never made a pancake in my life; I had no idea how to tell when they were ready to flip or when they were done, but I was up to the challenge. Besides, I'd look cool. The siblings would all wonder how they had survived without me. Customers would ask George where he'd been hiding me all these years, and he would beam with pride and wonder the same thing. He'd put his arm around me and say, "Oh, this is Julia. She's my baby."

I had to do well with pancakes. Doing pancakes would be my ticket off the bucket.

A little later, my father peeked over my shoulder to check my work, and I just about toppled over. He had a different look in his eyes, unlike the one he had when we had parked our bikes in the driveway. This expression was glassy, distracted, and a little possessed.

I showed him my bloodied fingertips, cut by shrimp tails that had poked my frozen skin—and then something happened.

He twitched. This was not your run-of-the-mill little eyebrow tick. I watched it develop, moving in stages, like a body skidding across the ice, or a ten-car pileup. His eyes closed, his neck swiveled, his right shoulder rolled, his knee jerked, and his foot kicked. Ammens, like tiny snowflakes falling from somewhere in his pants, floated slowly to the floor. At once amazed that his head was still attached and afraid that it might happen again, I thought, *What the hell was that?*

"Dad?" I said.

He just looked at my meager progress with the

shrimp. "You know, Grandma was slow, but she was old." He walked away.

I was too shocked for the insult to register. I had seen variations on "the twitch" before, like, every time someone put the milk carton back in the fridge with two sips left in it or when he found an errant spoon in the ice cream. But that day at brunch, the twitch had an intensity that sent a shiver down my spine. People's bodies were not supposed to behave like that unless they were wearing a straitjacket and buckled to a bed. And those people were heavily medicated. They could not possibly make soft-boiled eggs, or read *Stuart Little* with their eyes closed—could they? And what was that shit about Grandma?

Amy finally arrived with my chef clothes and took me to the employee bathroom to change. She kicked open the door and disappeared behind a wall of smoke before I got the chance to ask her about Dad's twitch. I followed. Waitresses stood before cloudy mirrors, pulling up skirts and nylons, tidying aprons, corralling hair by using bobby pin after bobby pin and gallons of Aqua Net. Cigarettes dangled from every lower lip. This was the dressing room, the inner sanctum. I was part of the club now, dressing among restaurant legends whose names I'd heard around the kitchen table—Margie, Marlene, Bernice, Gail, Sue, Geri, Willie, Lillie—names that commanded George's respect and therefore mine.

25

In short, these women were the front line. They took all the shit. This was their foxhole, and I had climbed in.

Don't cough, don't cough, I thought, trying to breathe with all that smoke, *or they'll never let you back in.* It was bad enough being the boss's kid—we were all marked—but I was the baby, soft and spoiled. Many of these women had been in that bathroom since before I was born. They had crust; I only had puncture wounds. Their chops, taut and sinewy, had been tested in some of the ugliest shifts in the industry: Easter Sunday, Father's Day, and the dreaded Mother's Day. My chops still had baby fat.

They watched me as I dressed, one eye closed behind tendrils of smoke, the other sizing me up.

Nothing fit quite right. The chef pants were too tight, squeezing my linebacker thighs, and way too long. And the chef coat, bright and crisp from the laundry, could have doubled as a shelter for a family of five. It was double-breasted, though, very cheflike. The size didn't matter. I loved the way it felt, buttoning one side over the other. I slid a brand-new bib apron over my head, folded it a few times, and tied it tight around my tummy.

The only thing missing was the hat. Headgear in most restaurants is much like the headgear in the Catholic church—each hat represents a distinction in the hierarchy. Tall chef hats, short chef hats, chef caps, baker's caps, baseball caps, bandannas, and hairnets usually indicate a person's position in the kitchen. We didn't stick to those formalities. George, being the leader, had a tall, white pleated paper hat. Everyone else, no matter where on the food chain, wore bandannas or baseball caps adorned with the restaurant's logo. I opted for the bandanna. The bandanna said you were tough enough to handle whatever the ride threw at you.

I looked in the mirror, turning this way and that, smoothing the outfit around my sides. Yes, I was the real deal.

MY FATHER SERVED the brunch from behind a giant chafing dish on wheels. We called it the eighteen-wheeler. Every Sunday it was rolled it to its designated spot in the dining room and plugged it in to an outlet. Stainless-steel pans filled with bacon, sausage, scrambled eggs, tenderloin tips, egg noodles, and the beloved whitefish sat elevated above simmering water and underneath three heat lamps. It was parked directly across from the pancake station. Next to the eighteen-wheeler stood a table covered and skirted with white linen. This was where the brunch-goers picked up their plates from under another heat lamp.

Amy gave me a quick lesson in the art of pancake making. Honestly, it was a snap. I wielded a swift spatula. My practice cakes were light, fluffy, and done to golden perfection. As customers approached, I asked them, "Blueberry or plain?" Simple.

George stood across from me, fidgeting with the serving pieces, placing them just so, running his hand along the stacks of plates every thirty seconds to make sure they were hot, and clicking a set of tongs with such rapid fire that they sounded like the camera shutters of a thousand paparazzi. *Click-click-click,* as if he were keeping time to some sort of schizophrenic beat in his brain. The twitch, and the big vein pulsing just above his glassy left eye, fell into perfect rhythm: *Click-click-click-click,* twitch, bulge; *click-click-click-click,* twitch, bulge. As I poured batter, blueberry or plain, onto the griddle, I wondered if this thing of his had a diagnosis. One of my brothers—Jeremiah, I think—had let me watch *The Exorcist,* and it looked to me like George and Linda Blair had the same problem.

Nothing stopped the brunch, though, not even demonic possession. I plodded along. It turned out that "doing pancakes" was fun for exactly six minutes. It's not that tough to get them right, again and again. There's a book out there about a guy who goes to heaven and plays so much golf that eventually he gets a hole in one every time he steps up to the tee. Perfection begets boredom. Talk to anyone at a cocktail party who got a 1600 on his or her SATs. That's what "doing pancakes" was like, minus the sense of superiority.

Outside, the temperature was a sweltering 95. The air-conditioning in the dining room didn't stand a chance against the steady tropical hiss excreted by the pancake batter, bubbling on a greasy griddle. It had to be 112 degrees where I was standing. It felt like I was on the equator. Everything stuck to everything. And my underpants, thick with humidity, had become an issue. Each bathroom break became a tricky twenty-minute battle between hurried hands, a fleshy bottom, and sticky, tangled cotton.

Because it had become so unbearably hot, I decided to keep a tall glass of ice water on the ledge next to me. It seemed like a good idea, it really did. I had just finished with a rush of pancake lovers. A thin river of sweat rolled down the middle of my training bra. My clothes felt fused to my body. I lifted my glass, the icy water just about to pour across my lips—

Then I realized that, across the room, George was watching me. My heart kicked up as if it were clothespinned to a bicycle spoke. Instinct told me I was about to be killed: death by tongs in front of three hundred brunch-goers.

He walked slowly toward me, the tongs, the twitch, the vein. *Click-click-click-click,* twitch, bulge. *Click-click-click-click,* twitch bulge.

He stopped in front of the griddle, gestured to

my glass with his tongs. He leaned over and whispered, in a gravelly voice sounding just like Linda Blair's, "Never, never eat *or drink* anything, ever, *ever,* in front of the customers."

His admonition set my lip quivering. Who the hell was this guy, and how did he get to be so mean? *Don't cry, don't cry, don't cry,* I told myself while I held my breath and squeezed back tears, and his look bored a hole in my psyche. *Jesus, please help me,* I prayed.

Then my father turned and walked away, the tong punishment avoided. It was a miracle—small, but a miracle nonetheless. Jesus saved.

A little while later, lips white with dehydration, I retreated to the kitchen, out of sight, to get a drink. Once there, I also realized I was starving. Oddly, you don't eat much when you work in a restaurant. If you do get to eat at all, it happens on the run. I spied a plate piled high with break-fast sausage, fresh out of the oven, glistening under the heat lamps on the cooks' line.

I listened for the tongs. Nothing; the coast was clear.

I pinched one sausage off the pile and tossed it from one hand to the other as I headed back to my pancake post.

We've all done it, taken a bite of hot, greasy pizza and burned the hell out of the roof of our mouths. The only difference with a sausage is that it's not just the roof that gets it: your entire mouth—tongue, cheeks, and chin—are instantly awash in hot, sticky liquid. The thing seemed to have life of its own, and the harder I tried to swallow, the hotter my mouth got. The sausage defied every attempt at consumption

A line was forming at the pancake griddle. *Shit. Shit. Shit.* For some reason, instead of saying, "Throw it away," instinct said, "Hide it." Sunday brunches come with messy waitress trays by the dozen, everywhere, piled high with china, glasses, and flatware used in multiples by customers visiting the buffet two, three, and four times. Not that day, though; certainly not that moment. Thoughts raced through my head: *Throw it against the wall; throw it on the floor; hide it, hide it, hide it, somewhere, quick.* My father's warning flashed through my panicked mind: *Never, never, eat* or drink *anything, ever, ever in front of the customers.*

Then I had an "aha!" moment. At twelve, instinct is underdeveloped. Foolish. You do crazy things, things you wouldn't do at perhaps . . . thirteen. I looked down, pried open the right pocket of my beloved chef pants, and squeezed the sausage in.

In a panic, certain things just don't occur to you, like, say, for example, the fact that something hot in your mouth is just as likely to be hot in your pocket. Chef pants are supposed to be heat resistant, but they don't say how resistant.

They don't come with a warning that reads: "Not to be used as a hiding place for breakfast sausage, stupid." It took a moment for the hot grease to soak through the cotton pocket and into the skin across my thigh. I let out an imperceptible little whine as I stepped behind the pancake station. I debated, but knew I couldn't take the sausage out. Those customers, waiting for their pancakes, would tell. My stomach churned. Tiny sweat beads clawed their way through the tight skin on my forehead and upper lip. The customers' faces wobbled before me, like they were staring at me from a fun house mirror, shrieking, laughing, and pointing. They knew. They would tell on me. And I'd be left alone to face the look, the vein, the twitch, and the tongs. It would mean shame for me and disappointment for my father. That sausage was an indelible black mark, my ticket back to the pickle bucket, back to the parking lot. After finally making the team, I'd be taking myself out of the game, just like that.

No, I decided, I couldn't let that happen. Some decisions we make and some are made for us. Either way, life leaves its little mark, defining us, before and after. I crossed over that day. I decided. I played through the pain, asking each customer with a whimper, "Blueberry or plain?"

2

Moving Days

We moved from Milwaukee to Cedar Grove in 1981, the summer between my fifth and sixth grades, and I took to sleeping in my parents' bed, something I had done when I was younger. I used to tell them I had bad dreams, but actually, thanks to my overactive imagination I'd end up freaking myself out in the middle of the night. My room had been upgraded from the walk-in closet, and now the white eyelet curtains hanging over my bedroom window took shape, and the maple leaves outside whispered in the breeze off the lake. A shadow on the wall became a slightly decomposed hand, and as soon as I saw the rusty pitchfork from the garage wobble in the knotty pine wall, I tiptoed to their bedroom.

This habit grew worse after our house on Prospect was robbed a few years earlier. I awoke to a hysterical screech and saw my mother, Terry, in her nightgown, pushing my father, in his boxers, down the hall after the burglar, who was wearing a pair of jeans and a T-shirt. He had taken the screen off one of the family room windows and had wandered up to my parents' room. When he pushed their door open, my mother thought he was just one of the kids. My father saw the man's shadow as he stood over my mother holding a screwdriver with a sixteen-inch shaft. The man said, "Where's your money?"

My father's wallet, oddly full of cash, sat on the dresser not two feet away, yet neither of them thought to hand it over. Instead, thinking the burglar had walked past each of our bedrooms and murdered us on his way, my mother let out an animalistic scream and my father leaped over her, chased the intruder down the hall and the stairs, and out the window.

Today I suppose the anxiety I experienced would be called posttraumatic stress disorder, including my habit of sleeping with Terry and George. Some parents would be encouraged to employ the help of a psychotherapist. Instead, my dad decided to pay me fifty cents for every night I stayed in my own bed. It worked, and it only cost him three hundred and eighty-five bucks. You do the math.

Cedar Grove was an unwelcome and costly change for our family. We continued to lock our doors, of course, even though the nearest bad guy would have had to pick his way through forty miles of corn, alfalfa, and soybeans.

Everything else, however, was different. The schools were public, the churches reformed. There was not one Jewish person to speak of, much less a decent matzo ball soup, nor did the town have a movie theater or a department store. It had a Main Street with a variety store, a bakery, a coffee shop, a Hardware Hank, and a set of railroad tracks that stopped pickup trucks on their way to the dump. The house—cold, damp, and musty—felt much more like a cottage. The gravel drive forced us to abandon shooting hoops and hitting tennis balls against the garage. And our only neighbors, Clem and Millie, looked like they had come over on the *Mayflower*.

George was a little bit country—his family tree had some awfully straight lines, after all—but not Terry. She was a city girl. Anything north of the Milwaukee County line represented the end of the world to her. Beyond that there be dragons. Her history lived at 4418 North Prospect, twenty-two years of it. She had dug in, twenty-two years of neighbors, phone calls, cocktail parties, borrowed cups of sugar, kids, friendships, cuts, trips to the emergency room, report cards, fund-raisers, visits to the police department—twenty-two years of sitting at the kitchen table, the tip of her cigarette glowing at all hours of the night, waiting for my siblings to come home.

Her life took shape around those memories of the house on Prospect; my father's, on the other hand, took shape around the restaurant. His history lived there, wading among a constant flow of cooks, bakers, dishwashers, waitstaff, bartenders, purveyors, and customers. With the move, my mother had to re-create everything anew in Cedar Grove. Dad had to re-create nothing.

In the end my father stomped his feet like a little girl and won the battle surrounding the move, but Terry was fiery Irish and stubborn German, so she never did give up the war. Johnny and Jimmy were gone. Katie, Peggy, Chrissy, Amy, and Stevie would all be in college in the fall. Five tuitions, two mortgages, and a nearly empty nest created a tipping point. Something had to give.

They struck a deal. George put the decision in her hands, stating that he would go along with whatever she wanted to do. For a few brief moments I believed we would stay in our house on Prospect Avenue, and our world would be righted after all. Whether or not she actually weighed the pros and cons remains a mystery. If I had to guess, I'd say her decision was made well before they shook on it, but I never asked, and she never said.

A week later, Terry sat at the kitchen table while my father leaned against the counter. I eavesdropped from the dining room.

"I want to stay here, George, on Prospect," she said. "We've been here over twenty years. This is the home the kids know. This is the home I know."

My father turned and stomped out the back

door. Foot stomping never worked in our family, so Terry's eventual concession left us all stunned.

UNTIL WE MOVED to Cedar Grove, and after that to Oostburg, I saw my parents as two separate entities, a mom and a dad, who were put on this earth for one purpose and one purpose only: to take care of us. Especially me. Of course, I understood that they were married, but to me, married just meant they slept in the same bed and took turns using the bathroom. The notion that they actually had a life separate from mine was as mysterious to me as high school later would be. It was a possibility, sure, but even though it was right there at the end of my nose, I didn't see it happening. They never showed us their marriage. If they fought, we didn't know; if they worried about money, we didn't know; if they had differing opinions about how to discipline us, we didn't know.

We saw a united front. Any ripples in their marriage, were, simply put, none of our business.

George's overruling of my mother's decision, and the subsequent move, created a ripple in our family, a little like the way the Colorado River created the Grand Canyon, only it happened overnight. It was the first time I saw my parents on opposite sides of anything, and they stayed on those sides for the next eighteen years.

Occasionally, they would meet in the middle, over their first brandy Manhattan, only to retreat, lobbing insults, halfway through the second. Grudges, even when held tight to the chest, bubble up; just add booze.

Because I was eleven when all this began, my opinion was completely irrelevant. It was as simple as that. Eleven didn't get an opinion. The chief weapon in my arsenal, foot stomping, had been stolen by my dad, so I was left with tears and pouting. Both were rendered ineffective when my mother shouted at me to snap out of it. Going up against Terry was pathetic, like throwing stones at a rocket launcher.

I watched and sometimes tagged along as Stevie and Jeremiah spent the entire summer driving load after load of the "small stuff" to Cedar Grove, where twenty-one-inch concrete Dutch boys and girls leaned in for a kiss on every single lawn. My mother's car, a 1977 forest green Buick Century, was loaded down repeatedly with stuff from the garage, the attic, and the wood pile from underneath the basement stairs, dragging it all north on I-43, the occasional spark spitting from the back bumper in its wake. If there was room, I sat in the backseat, where a wire poked through the vinyl binding. By the time we passed the historical marker on Sauk Trail, blood trickled down the back of my thigh.

Our family became tiny overnight. Jeremiah

and I, and Luke, Jimmy's German shepherd, were the only ones who made the move with Terry and George. Jeremiah made it through his freshman year at Cedar Grove High before my mother let him move back to Milwaukee where he could live with Jimmy and his wife, Treasie, and attend Marquette University High School. I hated him for that, plain and simple. I really did. I hated him for choosing to leave me alone with our parents. And I hated my parents for loving him more, for letting him go and forcing me to make change work.

So there you have it. Ugly, I know. The green-eyed monster had set the preadolescent pendulum in motion. The swing was nauseating for all three of us. During the day I walked along the beach, past the stagnant creek that ran like a river in springtime, toward the windmill beach. Choking back big prepubescent tears, I imagined my parents' faces and kicked sand in their eyes. I grew fangs and shrieked insults at my mother, the slave driver, for making me clean my own bathroom. I scolded my father for forgetting to bring home CheddarWurst from the Wednesday night buffet.

Then, at night, I crawled into their bed. What are you going to do?

JUST A YEAR and a half later, on a sticky July night, they decided to move again.

My mother finally accepted the fact that we were not moving back to Milwaukee. "But," she declared between drags of her cigarette, "if I have to live out here, I'm finding a house that *I* like."

The nerve.

So every Saturday during the fall of eighth grade, my dad and I loaded up the contents of the garage, the attic, and the wood pile from underneath the basement stairs, and drove another five miles north to Oostburg, population 1,647, home of the Flying Dutchmen, the name given the local high school athletic team. It was Cedar Grove all over again, except Oostburg had a corner tap.

Since we were moving only five miles up the beach, I thought they'd let me stay at my still relatively new school in Cedar Grove.

"Nope," my mother said. "You're switching to Oostburg after Christmas break."

"What?" Her words collided wildly in my brain. I had an awful taste in my mouth, like I had actually taken a bite of the bullshit sandwich she had just served.

"There's no bus to Cedar Grove, and I'm not driving you every day."

"What!" I buckled to the floor, driving my fists one after another into the carpeting. "Dad! Dad can take me to school. All you have to do is pick me up!" I sobbed. Sand and dog hair clung to my cheek. I saw a lonely Cheeto lost under the coffee table.

"No. It'll be easier this way."

"Easier for who? Easier for you! You only care about yourself. I can't believe this shit."

"Listen, Lady Jane . . ."

"Lady Jane" meant serious trouble. Lady Jane only came around when family heirlooms were accidentally dropped down the basement stairs, lady-head dimes were spent on Lemonheads and Mike and Ikes at the drugstore, and Dutch elm disease fungicides were ingested. Lady Jane usually received a swift slap across the face and a bar of Ivory soap to the molars.

"I mean it," she said. "This is *not* your decision."

I picked myself up, shuffled to my bedroom, and slammed the door.

I reached into my stockpile of rebellious behavior, growing smaller by the day, and pulled out the silent treatment. I didn't stand a chance against Lady Jane, but the idea of surrender made my ears ring and my chest tighten.

Terry would say, "I need you to do me a favor and pack up the cabinets down in the family room."

Favor! Favor! Pack your own damn cabinets.

Then she'd say, "I mean it. We're moving, missy, whether you like it or not, so snap out of it!"

Four months of this did nothing. The movers arrived the day after Thanksgiving. I lay on the couch, rigid as a fence post, and watched them dismantle my world—again. My chest heaved under the weight of my parents' meanness. I fired murderous looks at my mother, wishing she'd take one to the heart, grab her chest, and fall all over me in a flood of tears. Instead, she stood at the dining room table, smoked cigarettes, and told the movers to be careful with the Wedgwood lamp. A cloud of gray smoke mingled with the dust and sunlight over my head. I remember thinking my death would serve her right.

Begging my father to intercede on my behalf did nothing. Impervious to my tears, he knew an every-man-for-himself battle when he saw one—we all did. Delirious in my disbelief and due to switch schools the day after Christmas break, I decided to petition the Lord and received a disgustingly pustulant case of strep throat. Thanks much, Jesus. Even that didn't work; my mother assumed I was faking—which, in her defense, I usually was—and sent me to school anyway.

Terry and George had weathered the teenage storm eight times. They had the flashlights, the blankets, and the AAA membership; hell, they even had chains on the tires. At thirteen, like it or not, I was not in the driver's seat, I was along for the ride. And no way was I going to skid off the path. Come home late or not at all? Child's play.

Drink beer or smoke pot? Give me a break. Set fire to the garage or the house? It had all been done at least once before, if not six or seven times. Short of becoming a cocaine-using arsonist-hooker, there was nothing I could do to appear sufficiently damaged.

Thus, I was doomed to be the new kid yet again.

I PRAY THAT our system of streamlining kids in the public schools has improved since that first day I spent at Oostburg Middle School. What a circus. I started in the middle of the school year, and the strep was so bad I could barely talk, so the guidance counselor put me in the LD classroom. Back then, any kind of learning, emotional, or physical disability was labeled LD. I had no idea what it meant, but after a couple of hours, I figured naughty was as good a definition as any.

Kids threw whatever happened to be in their hands: gum, paper, pens, and every now and then, coins. One girl, a tiny bit of a thing with stringy blond hair and a budding case of acne, sprang up from her seat for no apparent reason and then sat back down again. She did this over and over, like a jack-in-the-box. And I watched the guy next to me carefully shear off the edge of his desk with a hunting knife longer than my arm. Departmentalization had not reached the

LD kids at Oostburg Middle School, so all classes took place in the same room, where nothing could be heard, much less learned, owing to the constant chaotic chatter.

The teacher, Mr. Janacus, also the eighth-grade basketball coach, had a front butt and boobs bigger than my mother's. I gave him the nickname Dr. J. He stood in front of the class, attempting to explain polygons while digging out his earwax with the lead of his mechanical pencil. I looked over at hunting-knife guy, started to open my mouth to crack a joke—something about "pick me a winner" or "digging for gold"—and then decided against it. I suspected there was a divergence between hunting-knife guy's sense of humor and mine. I sat back and settled into the loneliness of having a wisecrack and no one to share it with.

Later, jack-in-the-box girl came over and showed me two pictures. "Which one is a triangle, and which one is a circle?" She asked.

"What?" I shook my head, hoping I had mis-understood.

"Which one is a triangle, and which one is a circle?"

"Seriously?"

"Yeah."

I decided enough was enough. I looked over at Dr. J, seated at his desk, waved my hand, and tried to say, "Excuse me, Mr. Janacus, I don't belong in here," but nothing came out. My own voice had abandoned me. I panicked, and the wheels—the ones that kept my emotions from veering into hysteria—came off. Should I grab the hunting knife and shear off my own head? That would teach them.

I had a brain trapped inside a body, inside a room, inside a house, inside a town, and it knew the difference between a fucking triangle and a fucking circle.

I pushed the girl out of the way with my desk, got up, and walked to Dr. J's desk, placing one foot carefully in front of the other.

We're moving, whether you like it or not.

This is the way the ball bounces.

Where's your money?

You're coming to work the brunch with me tomorrow.

This is not your decision.

He sat, his fleshy breasts resting on his desk calendar and neatly hiding the last two weeks of January, eyeballing the waxy beige fruits of his labor on the tip of his pencil. Then it happened. Perhaps it was the fever, perhaps it was the Holy Spirit, could have been the boobs; I can't tell you, but I smiled. It was an inside smile, big, toothy, and soulful. Survival somehow made sense to me then. A fish out of water, I suddenly figured out how to breathe and found my voice. I looked Dr. J in the eye, stared down at his pencil, licked my lips, winked, and said, "You gonna eat that?"

3

Driving Lessons

Eventually, the house in Oostburg felt like home. Its previous owner had called it Cedar Dune because of the tall cedars in the back and the sand dunes out front. But we called it the lake house or the Oostburg house, as if we had other homes, in Galway and Martha's Vineyard.

Ours was the fourth house on Sandwood Lane, a dusty macadam under a canopy of birch, maple, ash, and beech, all stretching for a better view of Lake Michigan. The road opened into a small clearing with a patch of wiry grass the size of a cocktail napkin. Alongside the flagstone grew a thicket of aggressive ferns that come mid-July were tall enough to tickle my underarms. The place was a breeding ground for every creeping, stinging thing known to man.

My father's "workshop" was in the back too, attached to the garage. Since George didn't "work" in the handy-around-the-house sense of the word, not long after we moved in, the workshop turned into a basement, an attic, a second refrigerator, and a really cheap liquor store. George futzed around out there, drinking Manhattans and inventing truly frightening ways to murder the squirrels and raccoons.

Inside the house there were two levels, up and down. The dining room, living room and my parents' bedroom were up. Downstairs had two bedrooms (mine and the dorm-type room—the one with the four single beds, two cribs, and fireplace that we never used), George's office, and a "plant room." Nothing ever grew in the plant room after we moved in. There were grow lights, but we only flipped them on when we needed to find a bottle of the really good wine.

My room was directly below Terry and George's. Every night I heard them shuffling around, shifting and settling. I heard my mother draw the curtains, brass rings gliding across an iron rod. I heard my father drop his book on the floor and sixty seconds later begin to snore. They passed each other in the night, on their way to and from the bathroom. And in the morning, before the clanging of the dishwasher, I heard them mumbling. Sometimes I'd pull the covers over my nose, look up at the ceiling—more knotty pine—and wonder what they were talking about.

Terry kept house, quit smoking, took up knitting, quit smoking, and took up knitting again. She watched *The Young and the Restless*; *Murder, She Wrote*; and *Matlock* religiously. I went to school and made friends, again. George went to and from work, and as I had started doing shortly before we moved there, on Sundays I went with him.

SLEEPING WAS MY thing. Honestly, it still is. Most days I wake up thinking about when I can get back in bed. Since no one seemed to mind, when I was young I embraced a lovely two-nap-a-day style. It didn't last long, though. Kindergarten came along when I was four, so I had to cut back to one long post–*Mr. Rogers* siesta. In high school I had an eleven thirty curfew that I missed only once, and that was because of an unfortunate run-in with the Sheboygan County Sheriff's Department. In college I never once pulled an all-nighter, not even in a bar. If my homework wasn't done by ten thirty, I just didn't do it. Age has changed nothing. I have excused myself to go to the bathroom at hundreds of parties, grabbed my coat, walked out the door, and gone straight home to bed. If the pope were saying midnight Mass in my living room . . . well, you get the idea.

So my new Sunday mornings were just . . . brutal. Saturday night parties were tainted because I knew 6 a.m. and the Sunday brunch were just around the corner. Every week, come hell or high water, George pounded down the stairs, slapping his bare belly, burst into my

48

room, and whipped open the curtains, singing, "Rise and shine, daylight in the swamps." Then he started in with the Bee routine, pinching and buzzing, until I didn't know whether to cry or kick him in the head. Getting up was the only way to make it stop.

It was summer. I sat defiantly at the kitchen table. George had cranked the windows open, letting a warm breeze tiptoe through the screens. He wasn't careful about the way he dug his spoon into his grapefruit half, yet each section separated easily and popped up, perfect and juicy. He sucked it into his mouth and went on reading the *National Catholic Reporter*. Grapefruit. I hated grapefruit. It looked so deliciously sweet and tasty, especially when he sprinkled sugar on it. But it had bitterness too, hidden in each plump little bulb, a bitterness that made my tongue curl up into the back of my throat. I wanted to like it; I still want to like it, and every now and then I try it again, only to kick myself for knowing better.

On those mornings, I sat, arms folded across my chest, and silently ran through my stockpile of nondescript illnesses, wondering which one might save me from brunch and let me go back to bed: sore throat, stomachache, earache. The problem was that the same illnesses that got me out of school were never enough to get me out of work. Terry fell for anything because she wanted someone to hang out with. My father, on the other hand, needed physical evidence of disease and/or dismemberment. If I said I had an ear infection, doctor's note be damned, I needed to prove it with blood coming out of one, if not both, ears. I'm not talking about a trickle either. I had to be losing blood, from one orifice or another, at an alarming rate. Puncture wounds did not qualify.

I had settled into the new house and new school just fine, but occasionally the trip into Milwaukee and the restaurant left me with a heavy heart. At fourteen, those forty miles might as well have been forty thousand. The drive home was the worst. It was like having to leave my home on Prospect and my friends again and again, week after week.

I believe on my parents' wedding day, just after they took their vows and agreed to accept children lovingly, the priest looked at my father and said, "And will you, George, always agree to drive the shittiest car in the house?" It's the only explanation for the fact that, try as he might to ride to and from work in luxury, my dad always ended up tooling around in some dirty, rusted-out tin-can Toyota with a 180,000 miles on it, and the kids ended up driving the Audi with the leather interior, cruise control, power windows, and sunroof. "It's safer this way," my mother would say, and so George was stuck with the car that had no handle on the driver's-side door.

Before climbing in, I swept newspapers, muffin wrappers, and bottle caps off the passenger's seat. It smelled like a bag of dead kittens was somewhere in the back. Could have been rotten bratwursts—whatever it was had hair on it.

"What is that *smell?*" I asked, pinching my nose.

"What smell? I don't smell anything." George smiled at my discomfort as he started the car and headed down the gravel road.

"God, it smells like something died in here, Dad."

He chuckled. "Hee, hee, hee." Offending us in the olfactory department gave my father great pleasure. His nose could not register mustard gas, so he marveled at our sensitive abilities, as if being able to smell a rotten egg was unusual. He constantly stuck one thing after another in our faces and said, "Does this smell bad to you?" We were all under some perverse obligation to smell it too, even though we knew we might pass out and die.

"You'll get used to it," he said, laughing as I hung my head out the window.

We pulled onto the freeway. My father was "that guy" behind the wheel. He drove exactly twelve miles an hour under the speed limit at all times and always stayed in the passing lane because it was "less bumpy." He never checked his blind spot. He left his blinker on for extended periods of time. And occasionally, in an effort to save gas, he coasted until the car damn near came to a complete stop before again pressing the accelerator. He got the finger a lot.

I crossed my arms, lay my head against the window, counted silos, and wondered if it was going to rain or if the cows were just really tired.

"You want to listen to a tape?" he asked.

"No, Dad. *God.*"

The radio was not allowed. According to George, it was all "noise." Once in a while we listened to tapes of his choosing: bird calls, sermons from the apostle Paul, or conversational Spanish.

"What are you thinking?"

I closed my eyes and let out a faint whine. We played this game every Sunday. He had yet to win.

"Nothing," I replied.

"Nothing?"

"Yeah, Dad, nothing." I rolled my eyes and sighed. His cheerfulness on Sunday mornings made my temples throb.

"How can you be thinking nothing? Your mind is a complete blank? There's absolutely nothing there?"

"Yeah, Dad, there is absolutely nothing there.

It's just a white sheet of paper." *With a picture of me strangling you,* I mused.

"Amazing! I don't understand how you can possibly be thinking nothing. There must be something."

"No, Dad, trust me. There's nothing."

"Nothing? *Amazing.*"

"Nope."

This went on for five or ten miles before we fell into a peaceful silence.

"What time do you think it'll be on the clock when we get there?" he asked when we reached Port Washington, the halfway point. Game number two. At Brown Deer Road, where we exited to go to the restaurant, a digital clock hung outside the bank on the corner. So from twenty miles away we estimated the time to the minute. The winner was whoever guessed closest without going over. The prize was satisfaction.

I checked the clock on the dashboard and, knowing it was wrong, asked, "What time does your watch say?"

"Seven twenty-seven."

Who doesn't like a word problem first thing Sunday morning? Figuring he was going twelve miles an hour under the speed limit and we were roughly nineteen miles away, I guessed, "Seven fifty-one."

"I'll say seven fifty-five."

"Are you sure you want to go that late, Dad?

You can't cheat and start coasting on the freeway, you know."

"Oh, yeah, I'll stick with seven fifty-five."

I won. We pulled off the freeway at exactly 7:49 a.m. I actually smiled, so I guess he won too.

It was a typical clicking, twitching, and bulging Sunday, except that I got to "run" the buffet. The novelty of working the brunch had dried up and disappeared as quickly as the sausage burn scab on my thigh. In addition to picking up cigarette butts, peeling shrimp by the trainload, and doing pancakes, the brunch provided hundreds of other monumentally tedious, disgusting, and exhausting tasks. Everything had to be done dozens, if not hundreds or thousands, of times: eggs cracked, melons peeled, bacon cooked, juices poured. Depending on how busy it was, or how slow you worked, any given task could reduce your frontal lobe to the size of a mustard seed.

Running the buffet was one of the few exceptions. It was as monotonous as every other job, sure, but it came with autonomy. Basically I watched, and when the trays holding scrambled eggs, whitefish, sausage, bacon, egg noodles, and tenderloin tips started to look empty, I ran to the kitchen and brought out more. The timing was key. Bringing the food out too early or too late, or bringing out a stack of plates that were anything short of scorching, could cause a sudden onset of convulsions in George.

Running also meant I could cram an occasional bite of something into my mouth. There was no such thing as taking a break to eat. Those people who sat down and ate were feeble and weak. They were culled from the herd the same way the cheetah picked out the gimpy gazelle on *Wild Kingdom*. I had learned to eat on the fly, grabbing a strawberry here, a ham roll-up there. The challenge, of course, was to have it down the hatch before you heard the tongs. Jeremiah could eat an entire long john in a single bite.

And running meant I actually got to hear my father talking to customers. One day, he broke his own cardinal rule "The customer is always right." That is the rule except, apparently, when he or she is being a big fat pig.

The guy approached the eighteen-wheeler with his plate out and tried to grab George's tongs that were sitting in the bacon. He winced, dropped the tongs, and drew his hand back to his side. I saw a tiny sliver of a smirk slide across my father's face. He didn't like people messing with his serving pieces, so he placed them with their handles exposed to an invisible trail of steam creeping up and out from underneath.

"What can I get you, sir?" George asked.

"I'll have seven pieces of bacon."

"*Seven* pieces of bacon?" Twitch, twitch, bulge, *click. "Seven?"*

The guy looked over his shoulder, a little embarrassed. "Yeah."

"You can have four. If you want more after that, you can come back." George grew up during the Depression. It's why he held the tongs.

AT THREE THIRTY we climbed back into the Corolla. I rested a leftover long john on my knee and George squeezed a martini shaker of brandy Manhattans between his thighs. On the drive home we counted cars. Each week, instead of taking the freeway, we weaved our way north on the old Highway 32. George detoured through the parking lots of the Port Road Inn, the Nantucket Shores, Boder's on the River, the Ulao Inn, and Smith Bros. Fish Shanty. Counting cars was my father's way of keeping an eye on the competition, but it also let the state of the industry settle into his quieted, post-brunch brain. These squares of blacktop, some more crowded than others, provided tiny snapshots of the early evening eating habits of the North Shore customer.

At the FOSTER ROAD 1 MILE marker, he started to coast. Running the stop sign at the end of the ramp, he was able to maintain enough speed to make the right onto Sauk Trail *and* the right onto

Wilson Lima Road. That's roughly a three-mile coast, going at a pace slow enough to make Mother Teresa grind her teeth down to her gums. We crept to a complete stop at the crest of the small hill just beyond the freeway overpass, and George gave the gas pedal a tap to get us over the hump. I dug my feet into the floorboard until my hair hurt.

I couldn't stand it anymore. Something snapped. Afraid I might chew off my own tongue, I looked at him and said, "Dad, can I drive?"

He gave me a sly sideways glance, "Do you know how to drive a stick?"

"Dad, I'm fourteen. I don't know how to drive anything." That was not entirely true. A couple of times, when I was really little, too small to reach the pedals, Jimmy had put me on his lap and let me take the corners on Lake Drive. But I could see George's wheels turning toward an answer of yes, so I didn't mention that.

He pulled the car onto the gravel, got out, and walked around. Wide-eyed with disbelief, I jumped over the stick shift and settled into the driver's seat.

"Okay now," he said. "Move the seat up."
I did.
"Put your seat belt on."
I did. He didn't.
"Okay, now put your left foot on the clutch and

your right foot on the brake. The clutch is on the left, the brake is in the middle, gas is on the right." He put my hand on the stick, covered it with his own, gnarled and worn yet warm, and showed me, "First, second, third, fourth, reverse." Then he let go. "Okay, push the clutch in and put it in first gear."

I did.

"Good. Now ease your left foot off the clutch, and at the same time ease your right foot onto the gas."

The car lurched forward and died.

"It's okay, it's okay. Put your left foot on the clutch and your right foot on the brake and turn the key." The engine revved.

"Okay, now try it again." The car died eight times before I finally made a smooth transition into first, and second, and then third, and at last fourth. He nudged me, wearing an enormous grin, and said, "Getting started is the hardest, first gear. Once you get the hang of it, though, it's like riding a bike."

"Way better." I smiled, concentrating on the center line, hands at ten and two. Corolla or not, it was the open road, and I was on it. The freshly fertilized summer wind swept through my window and out his, carrying away forever the irritation of coasting. My heart raced on ahead as we blew past cornfields and bounced over the broken white bridge that marked the entrance to the tree line. It was the most exciting one-mile trip of my life. When we reached the turn onto our gravel road, the car sputtered to a stop. He climbed out and I climbed over.

He settled back, put the car in gear, looked me straight in the eye, and said, "Don't tell Mom."

I knew enough not to tell, of course. I just couldn't believe he said it. I'd heard those words hundreds of times before but never from him. Usually they came down the basement stairs with a bong in tow. Occasionally they left a fingertip in the kitchen sink and a spray of blood on the cabinets. But partnering those words with my father was something else. I didn't realize such a combination existed, but instinct told me it could be mined—to what depths, I wasn't sure.

So I shut up and shook my head no. I definitely would not tell Mom.

THE FOLLOWING SUNDAY, when I heard him coming downstairs, I was skipping toward the bathroom before he made it to the bottom step. I showered, dressed, and sat bouncing my knee with anticipation as he ate his grapefruit and read the paper. Not wanting to raise any red flags with Terry, I read the church bulletin and did my best to look lethargic.

Before we reached the end of the driveway, George smiled and asked, "What are you thinking?"

"I'm thinking I should drive."

He pulled off to the side of the road and we switched spots. He let me drive a little farther each week, adding the distance to the next stop sign, conveniently set exactly one mile apart, before we switched back. Then, on the fourth week, I made the turn onto the freeway and neither of us flinched.

Our "partnership," my windshield time, and Jesus forced me to a couple of realizations. The first was that my father's desire for me to learn to drive was greater than mine. Honestly, driving was a little like doing pancakes. The thrill of it didn't last long, but once I took over the chore, George was done. He was fifty-nine and ready to be a passenger. This made him a good teacher, patient and relaxed. He never used the imaginary passenger's-side brake that I'd seen him use on my siblings; instead, he read the paper. Plus, I was better at driving than he was. He put his trust in me not because I was worthy—what we were doing was illegal, after all—but because I was handy.

And second, my parents were old. It was that simple; sometimes life just is. With the exception of the occasional skirmish over the fact that we lived in Oostburg, all the jagged edges had been worn down. Unwritten, unmentioned rules developed right under our noses. They went something like this: I agreed to suffer through endless episodes of *Murder, She Wrote* and *Matlock*, and my parents, each unbeknownst to the other, overlooked—actually encouraged—things like truancy and driving without a license.

We played with fire every Sunday, growing more and more careless. In the morning I blessed myself at the holy water font hanging next to the back door, and then I grabbed the keys off the hook and skipped out to the car. George let me drive all the way, to and from. We both knew it was wrong, but the delinquency bond was too much for either of us to resist. Besides, I was fourteen; it never occurred to me how far the long arm of the law could possibly reach, and I can't say with any certainty that George cared—at least it didn't seem like he did. I weighed nothing beyond the fact that it was cool. I was more concerned with the long arm of my mother. If she found out, two things were certain: I'd never be allowed to get my license, and she'd ask for a divorce.

But it was cool, so . . .

Of course, it was all fun and games, all *Butch Cassidy and the Sundance Kid*, until the day he ruined it. Not for him, for me. Just like a father. Two or three months in, I pulled the car around the parking lot and waited. He popped open the door, lowered himself into his seat, shaker of Manhattans in one hand and the Sunday paper in the other, gave me a leveling stare, and said,

"Now, don't get pulled over. I can just see what they'd say in the newspaper. 'Restaurateur Arrested Drinking Manhattan While Fourteen-Year-Old Drives Car.' " Then he stuck his nose in the paper.

Arrested.

I realized then and there that we had entered the realm of "Those People"—as in, the ones you see on the news, as in, can you *believe* the stupidity of Those People? We were one speeding ticket away from receiving our *Deliverance* merit badge; the one with the picture of Ned Beatty on it, the badge that came with a pickup truck, an outhouse, a banjo, and revoked a lifetime of dental hygiene privileges. My father was "that guy"; his mug shot flashed before my eyes. He was grinning, of course. Then I saw him in an orange jumpsuit, sharing a cell with hunting-knife guy. Only hunting-knife guy wasn't a boy anymore—he was a man with yellowish eyes, a ruddy scar on his left cheek, and a wad of Kodiak in his lip. They were in a cell together. My father pulled out a copy of *Much Ado about Nothing*, pushed his glasses up on his Roman nose, and began to read. Then hunting-knife man-boy spat a thick stream of slippery brown spit dead center on page one.

I white-knuckled the steering wheel that day. It was more than just a piece of hard plastic beneath my sweaty palms, much more. In my hands, I held his license, for sure, probably his checkbook and his freedom, possibly his reputation and his business, and more than likely, his marriage. Sweat poured down my cheeks. I slowed the car to five miles an hour under the speed limit and set the cruise control. I'd been reduced to driving just like my father. I looked over at him.

George was fast asleep.

4

The Backstory

Of course, my parents didn't always have nine kids. Before any of us were born, before the brunch existed, Terry and George had parents, siblings, and lives of their own. Their stories came to us filtered through time, memory, and parental prerogative.

My father had three older sisters, Angie, Helen, and Violet, and a younger brother, Jack. His parents, John and Anna Pandl, immigrants from a village on the Austria/Hungary border called Porppendorf, landed at Ellis Island in the 1890s and somehow found their way to Milwaukee. Perhaps they had dreams of "America," like so many other immigrants; dreams of finding their way, their independence, and their fortune. Honestly, I have no idea what their dreams were.

I do know, however, that their reality ended up in a marriage, five children, and a restaurant called the Whitefish Bay Inn, which still exists and operates today as Jack Pandl's Original Whitefish Bay Inn.

There's something "old country" about the place, as if it were plucked from a hamlet tucked among the evergreens in the Austrian Alps. The windows, with flower boxes overflowing with geraniums and vinca vines, the log exterior, the lanterns flanking the front door, and the hand-carved wooden sign out front hanging from an iron rod, all look like something straight off the Getreidegasse. Throw a snowcapped mountain behind the place and you're waiting for Maria von Trapp to come skipping down the street, singing, guitar in hand.

The Inn, as we affectionately call it, opened in 1915 and attracted diners from all walks of life. Railroad workers, bricklayers, mayors, governors, and beer barons landed via steamship or railcar at the Pabst Whitefish Bay resort, then made their way across the street and bellied up to the bar. Today customers arrive via BMWs and SUVs, after cruising past iron-gated mansions. Famous for its old-world charm, its giant German pancake, and its dirndl-wearing wait-staff, it's still one of the few places in Milwaukee where they know how to pour a beer properly, in a clean pilsner with a thick head.

My father worked with his mother and brother at the Inn until she died in 1967, leaving him enough money to venture out on his own. Her death was the birth of his restaurant, George Pandl's in Bayside, while his brother stayed on at the Inn. Rumors still exist today regarding the relationship—and the split—between the two brothers. It was as simple as my father wanting a place of his own and as complicated as providing for two families—one with three children, the other with eight—on the income from one small restaurant. In the beginning, change brought a few bumps, as it always does, but in the end the brothers settled into a happy friendship inspired by healthy competition.

PANDL'S IN BAYSIDE sits just five miles north of the Inn, across from a strangely unused Baptist church and kitty-corner from the Schlitz Audubon Nature Center. In the industry the restaurant is considered big, seating roughly 225 people. The L-shaped dining room points northeast and is surrounded by picture windows looking onto a wooded lot. The place has been remodeled extensively a couple of times, but the windows have always remained untouched. The view they offer is sacred: women wearing Prada and dripping platinum guard their window tables as if just after the salad course, Jesus Christ himself will deliver the entrée.

The seasons bring the passage of time and wildlife. Maple, oak, and ash trees bloom and wither. Deer, raccoons, chipmunks, chickadees, robins, finches, and cardinals wander by, searching for food, looking in at the diners with curiosity. They provide a serene, picniclike atmosphere. Pandl's in Bayside has a heartbeat, a pulse; it breathes. It is our tenth sibling, my family's special-needs child, born in between Jeremiah and me, my father's first baby, his gift.

I KNOW VERY little of my father's father, except that he started a tradition that lives on almost one hundred years later and that in 1932, at the age of fifty, my grandfather fell to his death down the basement stairs of the Inn. The offending water pipe that his head met with also still exists and operates today.

My dad's mom, Anna Baumann, lived longer, so there's more to know about her. She died in 1967, three years before I was born. We never had the chance to meet, but she did leave me a solid inheritance. I discovered, after unearthing a pile of old photos, that my grandmother endowed me not only with her massive Hungarian arms and her stovepipe legs, but she also left me a tremendous set of cankles. She haunts me every time I dream of owning a really kick-ass pair of cowboy boots. Cankles, life has taught me, survive the test of time. They are part of one's

DNA—try all you like to get rid of them, they're not going anywhere. You might as well try raising the *Titanic* with tweezers.

Grandma Pandl was tough, buxom, and brawny. She spoke German. She was not the kind of grandma who took the grandchildren overnight and let them eat candy. Even in photos she's a little scary, not so free and easy with the smiles. The photos make me wonder what kind of weak, watered-down version of this earlier generation we really are.

She came to America from Austria when she was sixteen, traveling alone, taking the place of her older sister who was afraid to make the trip. Back then, millions of young people made that voyage—it's why most of us are here—but alone at sixteen on a steamship across the Atlantic? That took some chops. At sixteen, I whined if I couldn't take the car to school, or if our hotel room didn't have a minibar. After her husband's death, she raised five kids, alone, during the Depression. I've heard stories about the Depression, read a few books, seen some pictures, learning enough to know ours is a better time. I'm also told she drank three fingers of brandy for breakfast each day, straight from a tub in one swig, tossing it back like a merchant marine. The last time I drank three fingers of brandy, I mixed it with Diet Pepsi and promptly threw up all over Jerry Wostrack's front lawn.

My grandmother was no Martha Stewart. She did not cross-stitch or crochet afghans. My grandma was a bootlegger. Forced to sell her home and move the family to rooms above the Inn, and unable to make ends meet, she took to selling alcohol during Prohibition. She got carted off to jail now and then. (Okay, maybe she was just a little bit Martha.) One summer day, my father and two of his sisters sat out back behind the Inn, playing a game—probably marbles—when suddenly a paddy wagon pulled up in front. They abandoned their game, of course, and hurried over to peek through the slats in the fence. "It's Ma! It's Ma they're takin' away in the paddy wagon!" Violet exclaimed.

The village rallied around my grandmother, extending credit and posting bail. My father always said it was because she was a woman. He said if she'd been the one who fell down the stairs and my grandfather had been a widower, serving alcohol and not paying the bills, the Inn never would have survived. I suppose he might be right, but I believe it had more to do with her liver dumpling soup than chivalry. Sure, money talks, but food talks much louder.

There is one speckled black-and-white photo where my grandmother can be seen wearing a bittersweet grin, sitting atop a Harley-Davidson motorcycle in the front yard of the Inn. It hangs on the wall there today, just inside the back door, next to the coatrack. If not for the frock, the dark stockings rolled down around the cankles, and the loafers that look like they might have been owned by Ben Franklin, she looks quite comfortable on that motorcycle, as if she often went rumbling down the open road with the wind blowing worries off her face.

THE SHOT-PUTTER PHYSIQUE skipped a generation. As a kid, my father, born in Milwaukee, was wafer thin. He was a bony boy with cropped hair and dark circles under his eyes. He wore blousy shirts, baggy knickers, no shoes. According to him, he walked barefoot to school every day, uphill both ways, through ten feet of snow. He and his brother, Jack, went to St. Monica's grade school in Whitefish Bay. Tuition was unheard of at the time, so Grandma could afford to send her sons off to the priests and nuns every day for a dose of pre–Vatican II Catholic discipline. They received the sacraments under the watchful eye of the beloved cigar-smoking Monsignor Dietz. They received the rest of their education under the stiff ruler of crusty nuns. They left St. Monica's armed with the Catholic faith and Palmer penmanship.

High school was marked by World War II, and after graduation, George enlisted in the army. He was an infantryman and a radio operator, and it's safe to say he hated just about every minute of it.

The war was essentially over by the time he landed in France and made his way to Germany. He participated in one battle on the Ruhr River, where, he said, "The Germans gave up in a hurry." It was April 1945.

I'm grateful that it all went well. Grateful that my family was left with boyish letters about eating candy and ice cream until fillings fell out, playing poker and Ping-Pong at the Red Cross, sitting under cherry trees watching dark-haired German girls in red dresses hang silk stockings on the wash line, drinking cheap wine and expensive beer poured with a pathetic head, and standing guard in the rain, arguing politics with the random English-speaking prisoner.

George had the luxury of disliking the army for its food, politics, and bureaucracy and because it took him away from home, not because it forced him to kill. Though I never asked him, I suppose he was thankful too that he never had to take a life or give one. He knew others had afforded him the ability to simply witness, for the most part, the aftermath. Humbled, I believe, by the fact that his predecessors had paid the ultimate price, he never spoke much of the war.

Back home, George had his heart set on the University of Wisconsin at Madison, but there were so many GIs flooding college campuses in 1946 that he couldn't find housing, so he stayed home and worked for a year before deciding to give Cornell University a try. He inherited a little of Grandma's moxie. After being accepted to Cornell, he took the train to upstate New York without any formal housing set up. When he arrived, he dragged his army-issue duffel bag around Ithaca, knocking on doors until he found a room for rent. In contrast, my parents dropped me off at college three different times: once in Madison, once in Omaha, and once in Chicago. Schlep around town knocking on doors? I don't think so. Every time I went to college the Buick was loaded to the ceiling with sweaters, books, tapes, linens, and a bunch of other shit I just couldn't live without.

My mother's life ran parallel to my dad's all those years. They crossed paths a thousand times and connected, I guess, on one thousand and one. Terry grew up on Shoreland Avenue in Whitefish Bay, less than a mile from the Inn. She attended St. Monica's grade school, went to daily Mass, cherished the smell of Monsignor Dietz's cigar, and learned the Palmer method, all just one year behind my father. She had two sisters, Betty Lu and Dorothy, two brothers, George and Bobby, and a dog named Mickey. My mother was number four, sandwiched between the two boys. She grew up a tomboy and developed an impish charm that could disarm the devil.

Terry wasn't much for jobs, at least not ones that paid. She graduated from Mount Mary

College, became an occupational therapist, and got a job at a psychiatric hospital in northern Illinois, which, as she remembers it, was not a new millennium mental health facility. In fact, she called it two parts *One Flew over the Cuckoo's Nest*, one part *Psycho*. Whenever Terry spoke of the job, I laughed as if she were telling some ridiculous story about a complete stranger. Something about her working with the mentally infirm just never seemed right.

She stuck it out at the job for exactly eight weeks, throwing up every Monday morning. The breaking point was the day a sedated schizophrenic male patient escaped after ripping open the front of her blouse, scattering the tiny buttons across the tile floor and exposing her utility bra. She wasn't the type to sacrifice modesty, advances in mental health be damned.

Her father, also named George but affectionately known as Daddy, died of a heart attack at fifty-nine. Daddy, having the benefit of being dead, was forever eulogized, while her mother, Nana, because she lived, was often criticized. Life and death are strange that way.

Nana and I had the chance to meet on several occasions. Her skin, flawless even after eighty years, fit her round, childish cheeks like an old friend. She smelled of Emeraude. She arrived at our house on birthdays and holidays with a box of Russell Stover chocolates in one hand and her turn-of-the-century hearing aid in the other.

She had trouble remembering I existed. But I was the last in a line of twenty-three grand-children, so I couldn't really blame her. When I was eight, she was eighty-six. After school one afternoon, I hopped on my bike and rode down to visit her at the Shorewood Hospital. *Hospital* in those days was code for nursing home. It was April or May. There was a chill in the air, thick with the smell of the first grass clippings of the season. I coasted down Prospect Avenue with my coat open, letting the breeze glide down the front of my plaid jumper, excited about surprising my Nana. I tossed my bike in a bush outside, took the marble stairs two at a time, rounded the corner, and headed down the hall toward her cauldron of a room. The radiator threw off enough dry heat to bake a cake, but Nana sat in a high-back chair next to her bed, wearing a thick wool sweater around her shoulders and an afghan over her knees.

"Hi, Nana," I said, leaning in and planting a small kiss on her doughy cheek.

"Who's there?"

"Julie."

"Julie who?"

"Julie," I said louder, directly into the receiving end of her handheld hearing aid.

"I don't know any Julie."

"Yes, you do, Nana, it's *me*." I could see by her

73

vacant stare that she had no idea who I was, so I took a step back, hoping I'd come into focus, set my hands on my shoulders and said again, "Look, Nana, it's Julie."

"I don't know any Julie. You don't belong here." She stood up, grabbed me by the arm, and led me out the door. For a second I thought she might be right, and she was not my grandmother after all.

We shuffled down the carpeted hall toward the oval desk at the top of the stairs. I saw the look in her eye. She planned on turning me in. I caught a glimpse of the nurse on duty. In my mind's eye she looks like Nurse Ratched.

I shook my arm, looked my grandmother in the eye, and said, "Nana, it's me, Terry's daughter." She and my mother had the same full face, the same smooth and satiny white Irish skin, and the same blustery gray-green eyes.

"I don't know you," she said.

Wobbly tears of invisibility bulged over the corners of my eyes, hugging my nose as they slipped down my own silky skin. "Nana."

Then she stopped, looked down, and laid her thick fingers on my cheek. "Oh, Julie!"

"Yes." I let out a deep sigh.

"Julie! You're Terry's daughter." She took my hand in hers and led me back down the hall as if nothing had happened.

It's about time, I thought, rolling my eyes.

74

I still feel like the anonymous Pandl at times, even now, the one who looks like the rest but nobody remembers. Whether it's your grand-mother turning you in to the nurse on duty or the Sheboygan County Sheriff's Department chasing you down the beach, being what's-her-name has its advantages, believe me.

5

Bon Appétit

It's true what they say about the shoemaker's child never being properly shod. While the restaurant brunch was a heavenly extravaganza, the food in our home refrigerator was mostly rotten—not completely, but mostly.

My father was very careful about what he served the restaurant customers. Their food was perfect: fresh, pretty, and delicious. Our food at home, though, was big, grayish brown, frankly a little scary. Nothing ever smelled quite right. Things liquid, like milk and juice, were thick and lumpy, and things usually chunky, like tenderloin tips, managed to break down and become brown, green, and viscous.

The only notable exception was beer, which in our house was a food group. My father enjoyed a head on his beer the way most people enjoy breathing. The perfect pour was a work of art, as in Michelangelo's *David*, only slightly more awe inspiring. In other people's homes or in other restaurants, he tolerated a lifeless pour in a dirty pint glass, but on his own turf it had to be served in a squeaky-clean frosted pilsner, stein, or even wineglass, and it had to have a thick, foamy head, ready to slip over the rim. Beer had to be pretty. An imperfect pour was a disaster, as in the Bubonic Plague, only slightly more frightening.

So my siblings and I, and our friends, approached everything in the fridge except beer with trepidation. You didn't just grab something and stick it in your mouth. This I learned at age four, after I popped a ham roll-up in my mouth and, while leaning against the open refrigerator door, promptly threw up on the kitchen floor. Eating in our house was a process. First, food was eyeballed with an attempt to identify; then it was smelled and, finally, rinsed, scraped, or cut.

Our food came home not through the normal grocery store channel but via the backseat of my father's car. Eggs came by the flat of thirty; cheddar cheese came in a ten-pound block; cottage cheese came in a five-pound white bucket; tenderloin tips, spaetzles, red cabbage, and curried chicken drummies came in glass gallon jars. Our hamburger patties did not arrive frozen in neat packages with appetizing pictures and nutritional information; no, ours had been removed from the back of the refrigerated drawer on the cooks' line, wrapped tightly in bloody plastic wrap and tossed in a Becker meat box next to a bunch of celery, a pint of strawberries, a few pieces of crusty cheese, a pile of loose mushrooms, and a stack of invoices that needed filing. And everything weighed a ton. I used a wagon to move the summer sausage from the fridge to the cutting board; the same wagon was used when the neighbor kids borrowed our gallon of maple syrup.

At home, my father enjoyed the sport of trying to slip rotten food past unsuspecting persons and creatures. Depression-era desperate to have food consumed rather than thrown away, he toyed with recipes. He tried to re-create my mother's macaroni and cheese using crinkle-cut clumps of moldy, unmeltable mystery cheeses leftover from the Wednesday night buffet. He put ancient Vienna beef hot dogs that he found in the back of the freezer in a batch of beautifully fresh spaghetti sauce. When no one fell for it, he retrieved the hot dogs, along with a box of waffles he'd recovered during the same freezer expedition and nailed them to a tree outside the kitchen window. We learned to be very careful about what we put in our mouths, but the birds and squirrels were on their own.

Even houseguests were not safe. George and I busied ourselves in the kitchen at the Oostburg house one night while my mother and her best friend, Ellen Noonan, sat chatting in the living room. Katie was downstairs switching a load of laundry. Dad opened the upper oven and said, "Whoops."

"What?" I looked over.

His brow furrowed in a brief moment of hesitation. Then he clicked his tongue in his cheek as if to say, *Oh well* . . .

"What?" I asked again.

"The chicken wings from last night," he said, staring in the oven. "I put them in here when we were cleaning up and I never took 'em out." He looked at me and raised his eyebrows as if to ask permission and then smiled.

"No, Dad."

He closed the door, turned the oven on, and chuckled quietly.

"Dad, you can't. Mrs. Noonan—she might get sick." I guess my mother was already immune.

"Oh, c'mon, don't be ridiculous, they're fine. I'll turn the oven up and kill anything that's in there."

"Dad, no."

"Ah"—he raised his finger—"don't say another word."

Katie brushed past me a few minutes later and I whispered, "Don't eat the chicken wings." But Mrs. Noonan, like the birds and the squirrels, was on her own.

Occasionally food items passed the eyeball and smell tests with flying colors, only to fail miserably upon hitting the taste buds. George made me a rib-eye one night when my mother was out of town. A hint of suspicion crossed my mind when I saw only one steak in the sauté pan, surrounded by a pile of soft mushrooms and sweet onions. But the thing looked and smelled so delicious it immediately put me at ease.

"Aren't you eating?" I asked.

"No, I'll eat later."

"Do you want part of that steak? I can't eat the whole thing."

"No, no, it's okay. Just eat what you want and I'll eat the rest later." *Just eat what you want*—another big red flag.

But I only shrugged and went into the sunroom to grab a TV table.

My mouth watered. He had seared the meat to perfection—dark brown on the outside and pink and juicy on the inside—placed it on the heated plate just so, with the onions and mushrooms spilling down at six o'clock, and sprinkled it lightly with seasoned salt and pepper. He even garnished the plate with a sprig of parsley. "Wow, Dad, this looks amazing. Thanks."

"You're welcome. Bon appétit," he said as he sat down to do his paperwork.

It cut like butter—a little too buttery for a rib-eye. I speared a forkful of the steak along with a mushroom and a few onions, popped it in my mouth, and knew instantly that something was amiss. It was like chewing the gauze off a festering open wound. The onions and mushrooms did little to disguise the noxious flavor as the meat slipped down my throat. I looked over and saw my father watching me.

"Dad!" I yelled, gagging.

"What?" He raised his eyebrows and shoulders, trying to look innocent.

"How old is this steak?"

"Well," he said, "it's got a little age on it." He chuckled.

"Ugh." I spit out the bit still in my mouth. "Seriously, you're laughing? It's not funny."

"Oh, c'mon, it's not that bad. Don't be such a baby." He laughed again. "What do you think they did in the covered-wagon days?" George loved to throw the covered-wagon days at us, as if he had single-handedly pioneered the West.

"Honestly, Dad," I said, wiping my tongue with my napkin. "Did you have to *save* it from the covered-wagon days?"

He never learned. Once, a few weeks after Easter, I caught him peeling eggs that had been boiled and dyed on Good Friday and used as part of the centerpiece on the dining room table. "What are you doing?" I asked. Of course I knew, but I desperately wanted to be wrong.

"Making egg salad."

"No, Dad, you can't."

"What do you mean, I can't? Why?"

"Those eggs have been sitting on the table for weeks."

"These eggs are perfectly good. There's absolutely nothing wrong with them. Look." He held out one that he had just peeled.

"It's pink." I fumbled through his finished pile and picked up another. "This one's purple."

"So?"

"So, you don't think anyone is going to be a little reluctant to eat rainbow-colored egg salad?"

"So what? A little dye's not gonna hurt you. Gad's sakes, you kids, how do you think the West was won?"

"I think, maybe, they didn't have time to dye eggs when they were busy winning the West." I walked away. No warning required on the egg salad. Anyone stupid—or blind—enough to eat that had it coming.

All these peculiarities in the food department ironically created a family of adventurous, unfussy eaters. How this happened remains a great family mystery. Instinct, survival, hunger—who knows? One would think that we'd be skittish around food, but we respected it, no matter how it smelled, whether it was veal saltimbocca, pheasant under glass, or some petrified nugget found hiding in the butter.

Food was sacred, not to be toyed with or thrown away. We discussed it, complained about it, and even cried over it, but somehow we knew it was bigger than a basic necessity. Food did much more than satisfy our appetites. It put a roof over our heads and shoes on our feet, sent us to private school, and paid for college. Sure, we all hid our fair share of gray tenderloin tips under the radiator against the wall, but eventually food taught us the basics: how to entertain, how to clean up after ourselves, how to behave. It worked.

That's as simply as I can put it. Rotten, fresh, messy, pretty—it didn't matter: my family came together around food.

6

Goddamn It, Jeremiah

As a family approaches double digits, chaos happens. It's inevitable. Somewhere around the fifth or sixth kid, parents completely lose control. Mine did. They showed no signs of surrender; there was no white flag, only big brown drinks. Then they disappeared.

Survival was the key word for all of us. I have no idea how any of us managed it, as life in our house was an every-man-for-himself scenario. You never revealed a weakness, such as thumb-sucking or bed-wetting. God forbid you developed acne or BO or put on a few pounds. You'd never hear the end of it. One well-placed blackhead could render a fairly healthy self-esteem paralyzed for months, even years.

Memories of growing up are chaotic. They're mental snapshots, really, random, not linear at all. I remember stepping off the curb in front of our house on Prospect Avenue; the screech of tires; the iron grill of a car so close to my face I could lick it; the gray hair, green eyes, and ashen face of the woman behind the wheel; my mother's knee pressing into my stomach and her right hand slapping my bare butt. I remember throwing up stuff—vegetable soup, chocolate chip cookie dough, Rice Krispies treats, salami and cheese and tenderloin tips—sometimes on my bedspread, sometimes on the bathroom floor, inches from the toilet. I remember sitting on a lap at the kitchen table while the friend of one of my siblings tried to teach me how to smoke. I remember being afraid the ash would burn my blankie. I was a chunky baby, with thick thighs, like loaves of French bread, and I had wispy, dark brown hair, eyes almost black, and big full lips.

I remember all these things, but because I was number nine, there is almost no actual proof I even existed. The family camera only came out for children numbers one, two, and three; after that, it was either broken or simply forgotten. It's a little like I fell out of the sky at age twelve. The few baby pictures that exist were all taken on the same day, as if someone said, "Let's get a few pictures, just in case she's kidnapped." In them I'm sitting in front of the TV, I have dirty hair, and I'm eating a huge bowl of mint chocolate chip ice cream, wearing a dirty onesie and a dirty bib that reads I'M A LITTLE BADGER.

Perhaps I *was* kidnapped.

THE FIGHT BETWEEN Jeremiah and me lasted twelve years, nearly driving the entire family to the brink of insanity. Why it lasted so long remains a mystery, but as self-respecting Roman Catholics, we now both blame our parents, of course. The feud touched every person who entered our house, though—friends, relatives, neighbors, dates, and future in-laws. Only the brave ones stayed. The others left, a bit emotionally scarred, wondering how such brutality would shape up down the road.

Born less than three years apart, we look the same, Jeremiah and I: same lips, same hair, same eyes, same thighs. Even today we are occasionally mistaken for twins, although he has slightly less hair than I do, and I have slightly larger thighs. By the age of nine, his bare feet produced a Limburger-like smell that could clear a room. He ingested small change, screws, and turpentine. The phone number for the poison hotline was on a green sticker attached to the phone above my mother's desk. The ipecac was underneath the kitchen sink, right next to the silver polish and the bleach.

The problem in the relationship between Jeremiah and me was simple: I existed.

"Put her down," he demanded, the day my mother brought me home from the hospital. "I want to play with her." Terry had been around the block enough times to know that "play with her" was toddler talk for "wrap my hands around her neck, sit on her head, and smother her with my diaper." My presence had knocked Jeremiah off his baby throne, and he was pissed.

With very few weapons at his disposal and determined to exact revenge, he took to spitting in my crib. He would stand at the kitchen door and eyeball me from across the room, swaying back and forth on his high white shoes, blankie in one hand and bottle in the other, pretending to be mesmerized by the sunlight bouncing off the chandelier that hung above the dining room table. He waited until the coast was clear and then toddled over to the antique white crib my mother kept in the opposite corner, his poopy diaper and sourdough thighs stuffed into a pair of short pants. He couldn't fit his pudgy hands through the crib's wooden slats, thick with eighty-seven years of white paint, and he was too short to reach over the top, so choking me was out of the question. But with his face and mine just a few inches apart, he hawked up what little spittle he could, pursed his plump lips together, and took a shot. I'm told his aim was dead-on.

Katie acted as my bodyguard until I was about four, taking me all over town. For the most part, we went places where she could smoke cigarettes without getting caught. When I was small, she tossed me in the rickety old baby buggy, but eventually I graduated to the babyseat on the back of the family tandem bike. There was never anyone in the middle seat, just her way up front and me way in the back, twisting in the wind, no shoes, probably no clothes, certainly no helmet, just the "I'm a little badger" bib. Other kids brought fake babies to school show-and-tell; Katie brought me.

Other kids had their mothers register them for kindergarten; Katie did that. My mother couldn't bear the thought of bringing yet another kid to Lake Bluff School, so she had Katie do the job. But when one of the other kindergarteners asked her if she was my mom, she abandoned me, and I ended up back in Jeremiah's hands.

That's how the chaos was managed in our family: the next oldest kid took care of the younger one. It was a perfectly acceptable arrangement. Everything Jeremiah did, I wanted to do. It didn't matter if it was mundane, exciting, illegal, or even life threatening—I wanted in. If he played Little League, I wanted to play Little League. If he got to go camping in the Boundary Waters, I wanted to go camping in the Boundary Waters. If his hero was Chester Marcol, my hero was Chester Marcol.

The only wrinkle was the fact that given opportunity without consequences, we wanted to tear each other's eyes out. My mother, in one of many desperate attempts to move our fights anywhere but near her, forced us down into the basement. Basements have come a long way since the seventies. For starters, they have heat. They have dropped ceilings, wood paneling, soft carpeting, comfortable chairs, and flat-screen TVs. Our basement on Prospect Avenue was like *Heart of Darkness*, except I suspect the Congo was warmer and more welcoming. The stairs were mismatched two-by-fours held down with rusty nails. When the lights went on, centipedes the size of sheepdogs scurried across the gray concrete floor. Occasionally they materialized in the corner of the stairwell, where the ceiling met the wall. I'd sit on the top step in my nightgown and fire thick rubber bands off my finger in an effort to thin the herd. My sister Amy actually drew a picture of one and hung it on the refrigerator. "The horror! The horror!"

The basement's furnace room, and the furnace

itself, were straight out of Dante's seventh circle of hell. Things that went missing in the house— retainers, diamond rings, car keys—were declared to be "downstairs behind the furnace." Which meant they were gone forever and quickly forgotten.

My mother did laundry down there, and my father had a workshop, although he never once used it. There was a splintered worktable, with a vise purchased during the Dark Ages bolted to one end.

That vise sparked the invention of what I like to call the "here, Julie" games. One day, after Terry caught us giving each other snakebites in the family room, Jeremiah and I found ourselves tiptoeing barefoot across the laundry room and into the workshop.

"Here, Julie," he said. "I'll put my hands in the vise and you tighten until I tell you to stop."

"Then what?"

"We'll see how tight we can get it."

"Okay." Honestly.

He pressed his hands together like he was making his First Holy Communion and set them between the jaws. I grabbed the cold steel bar from underneath, cranked it around, and let it slip down the shaft where it landed on the end ball with a *clank*. I did this over and over again—crank, slip, *clank;* crank, slip, *clank;* crank, slip, *clank*—until his hands were waffled in nice and tight.

"Try to get out."

He set his feet and pulled with all his weight, shifted positions, and pulled again.

"Ha, I got you."

"Yeah, it's pretty tight. It feels kinda weird. Now let me try you."

" 'Kay." I danced with delight as I loosened the grip, anxious for my turn.

We switched places and he started to crank away, except he didn't let the rod slip and *clank;* he spun it around with speed and determination. I felt the jagged teeth sink quickly into the backs of my hands.

"Ow! Ow! Ouch!" I screamed.

He cranked again and smiled.

"*Ouch!* Goddamn it, that hurts."

"There, try to get out."

I wasn't all that tall. My stance gave me very little leverage, so I leaned back and felt metal bite my skin.

"I can't do it. Let me out."

"No."

"What?"

"No."

"What do you mean, no? I let you out. Let me out."

"No." He smiled and started to back out of the room.

"Agh! No, come back. Let me out, let me *out!*"

I squirmed. My pulse quickened and blood

pumped painfully, rhythmically, into my finger-tips. They turned bright red as I heard my brother bouncing up the stairs. I stood there and cried for what seemed like days while whispers of things floated across my feet. I can't tell you who finally came along and sprang me, but I can tell you that I marched directly up to my mother and showed her the evidence of my imprisonment: red-striped, flattened hands and purple finger-tips. I can also tell you that Jeremiah received so noisy a spanking when my father got home that I actually felt guilty. Tattling was bad form, no matter what.

Sometimes things got out of hand and accidents happened. But when blood was drawn, Jeremiah and I became allies. The sight of blood, his or mine, was immediately followed by the words *Don't tell.* Nine times out of ten, the words applied to Terry, but the inference included anyone within earshot who was older than us. We both knew that blood meant big trouble. Blood meant somebody would actually have to go find a Band-Aid. A Band-Aid in our house was a little like the Holy Grail: one existed, sure, but no one knew where. And when the box was found, the bandages disappeared so fast that our parents took to rationing them as if they were strips of bacon and we were at war.

"Here, Julie," Jeremiah said one rainy morning, after Terry caught us taking turns

90

socking each other in the shoulder and sent us upstairs to play. "You jump up and down on the end of Mom and Dad's bed and I'll try to knock you down with Mom's pillow."

Terry slept on a standard-size down pillow, rendered formless with age, stuffed inside a king-size pillowcase decorated with faded yellow daisies. We could get a strong grip on the empty side of the case, and the pillow was soft enough to wrap around two ankles, so it served our purpose too. The bed, a twenty-fifth anniversary present from George, had no footboard, only a long oak headboard with thick carved spindles on either end and one in the middle.

"Okay." I climbed up and jumped as high as I could, lifting my knees to avoid his swing.

Because the mattress was brand new, it had a good bounce. I was able to spring up with lightning speed. The idea was that the swinger, the one who held the pillow, had to knock the jumper off his or her feet, onto his or her butt, and then we'd switch places. Jeremiah was bigger than me, of course, so tripping him up in the loose sheets was oftentimes the best I could manage. He, on the other hand, could hook my ankles and upend me with the slightest tug.

I jumped as high as I could, maintaining balance by holding my arms out to the sides and rotating. He swung and missed, swung and missed. I couldn't help but giggle as the motion tickled my tummy and the pillow grazed the bottoms of my feet. The air caught my T-shirt as I drifted down toward the mattress. He clipped me once on the left, and again on the right, but somehow I managed to land and bounce again. Emboldened, I took my eyes off him for a second, reached up and back, and tried to touch the ceiling. I felt a sudden jerk forward as the fabric wrapped itself around my ankles. Then he let go. In his defense, gravity and physics did the rest. The ceiling drifted slowly past like a smoggy cloud as I floated backward. I had time to notice the chipped paint on the wall, just above the wooden bust of Jesus with the Crown of Thorns that my father kept high on his dresser. I'd like to say it was the face of Jesus that took my breath away, but really it was the impact of my spine against the not-so-rounded edge of the headboard's middle spindle. My butt landed dead center, in between two king-size pillows, in the space where my mother kept hers, and I felt a trickle of blood slide down the back of my underpants.

Both as white as ghosts, we exchanged the same terrified look.

"Don't tell," he said.

I choked on a few tears.

"Are you okay?" He scrambled across the bed. "Lemme see, lemme see."

My legs still tangled among the sheets, I rolled

to the side. He lifted my T-shirt and sucked in a quick stream of air between his teeth. "Jeez, I'm sorry."

An unsolicited, unforced apology was definitely a bad sign. For a brief moment I thought I might be dying.

"It's okay, it's okay. You're fine. Don't tell, though. Just don't tell Mom."

"I won't," I said, whimpering, and crawled off the bed and into my parents' bathroom. I climbed onto the radiator and checked the wound in the medicine cabinet mirror. The spindle had peeled a hefty chunk of skin off my back, leaving a hole about the size and color of a plum. I have no clear memory of how we solved the problem, but I believe it involved wadded-up toilet paper and masking tape. Make no mistake, my father made plenty of attempts at rationing toilet paper and masking tape, but the job was just too damn big.

Neither of us told.

Jeremiah's blood spilled too. Usually by his own accord, though. When we lived in Cedar Grove, one night he dragged me into the kitchen. He peeled a banana and held it in his left hand over the kitchen sink. "Watch this," he said, holding an eight-inch chef's knife in his right hand, drawing it back behind his shoulder like he was getting ready to split wood. "I'm gonna slice this banana so fast that it'll stick together."

"Okay." Honestly?

One swift swing and blood squirted every-where—out the screen and on the window, all over the knotty pine cabinets and the wrought-iron handles—and spilled into a saucepan that had been left in the sink.

He quickly grabbed the ever-present dirty and damp dishrag off the middle of the sink, wrapped it around his finger, screamed, "Don't tell!" and ran downstairs. I followed. When he finally peeled off the crusty rag, the blood flowed down his arm in measured pumps and his fingertip was gone.

This time, though, I had to tell. Missing appendages were a little harder to hide than holes in the back.

Occasionally, and oddly, friendship smiled on us along the way. Jeremiah taught me how to watch football: how to read a draw play, how to spot an illegal block in the back, and how to see when the offense was offside. He taught me how to hide in the bushes when the UPS truck stopped, wait for the driver to exit the sliding side door, run around the back, hop up on the knobby steel bench and hitch a ride around town.

He also taught me how to skeech. The word has several meanings these days. In our world it meant to sneak out behind a car driving down an icy street, squat down, grab the bumper, and skid along until you either let go or fell off. Skeeching happened on our winter walks home from school.

It required a small stature, so as not to be spotted by the driver; boots with absolutely no traction, so you could get a good skid going; and dry mittens that were not attached to each other with a string, or to the cuffs of your jacket with clips. Wet knit mittens adhered to a frosty bumper immediately, and any kind of clip or string producing even the slightest tug could beget an unfortunate meeting of tiny teeth and hard steel or of short legs and thick tires. Jeremiah would toss my clips into snowbanks and make sure my mittens were dry.

Befriending your enemy has the true and lasting beauty of a thing hard won. When concessions are made, bonds are formed. Our friendship knitted itself tightly around the scars we inflicted upon each other. It understood precise weaknesses, fears, and anxieties; it had the ability to expose, and even flaunt, but instead it chose to downplay, cajole, and create a binding strength.

It still does. Sure, he would have told me I looked fat in it, but I knew he would give me the shirt off his back. It's true that much of the time we found ourselves tangled, and sometimes strangled, in the rope of sibling rivalry, but time had its way of undoing the knots. Time, as is almost always the case, had its way of showing us the way.

So when Terry and George let Jeremiah move

from our new home in Cedar Grove back to Milwaukee, I was truly heartbroken. It was another unwelcome change. My friend and my foe were both gone, instantly, in the name of a Catholic education. My tether, twisted as it was, had become threadbare, its only remaining connections being my aging parents and the restaurant.

AFTER JEREMIAH MOVED back to Milwaukee, I encountered him only on Sunday mornings, where we shared a mutual disdain for working the brunch, although I believe circumstances may have made his dislike for it slightly more intense than mine. I remember one day in particular because it was at that brunch that he earned a nickname that stuck with him for years. It was in December 1983. It was a Packers/Bears game day and the Christmas decorations were up. The stuffed Frosty the Snowman sat shoved next to the TV in the dark and dusty southwest corner of the bar; his carrot nose, listless with age, hung over the right corner of the screen.

The brunch shift began at eight o'clock sharp. Like I said, death and/or dismemberment were the only real viable excuses for being late, especially for Pandls. At three minutes after, George, readying a box of beef tenderloin for trimming and sensing that someone was missing, looked around and shouted to no one in particular, "Goddamn it, where's Jeremiah?"

Twitch. No one answered. Everyone, including George, knew he lay less than five minutes away, cocooned in his flannel sheets at my brother and his wife's house, distilling the dark room with his Saturday night breath.

"I swear, that kid," George said, shaking his head while deftly sliding his boning knife under the silver skin of his first tenderloin. His work had a delicate rhythm that brought a strange smile to the twitch. He was able to lose himself in the simple task of perfect preparation and enjoy the immediate fruits of his labor. Tenderloin did not talk back, and it did not hide a jug of wine behind the garage. Setting the skin aside, he ran his left hand smoothly back and forth over the scarlet meat, searching for any small stray strips. He sliced off both tips, set them in an empty cottage cheese bucket, laid the trimmed meat in a stainless-steel steam-table pan, and picked up another.

A few minutes later I heard the back door slam, followed by Jeremiah's loafers slipping one by one up the stairs. He flipped a wad of dark, greasy bed-head hair off his face, revealing a gray pall covered with random shadows of teenage stubble, and red eyes, glassy and wandering, like marbles looking to squeeze themselves out of their thick misery and bounce back down the steps. His clothes—a wrinkled white oxford shirt, a pair of Levi's worn through at the knees, no socks, and a navy blue down ski jacket with a rip in the left shoulder—had undoubtedly been recovered from a pile next to his bed. He held his chef jacket and pants in a crumpled ball under his armpit.

"You're in deep shit," I said when he finally pulled himself up the last step. "Dad's already looking for you."

I could tell it was a monumental feat for him, just getting up the stairs; speaking was out of the question. We all knew what it took to get through a brunch shift under the best of circumstances, and mercy flowed freely among the staff on Sunday mornings. As lovely as the brunch smelled when you were well, a hangover (as I myself would learn later) could set your stomach spinning and your brain throbbing like the Zipper at the state fair, the difference being that ex-con carnies ran the rides at the fair and George ran the ride at the restaurant.

"Goddamn it, Jeremiah!" my father bellowed.

Jeremiah winced as if a knitting needle had been jammed into his ear. I giggled, sympathetically, but I giggled. There was something so awkwardly hilarious about hearing my father swear that way at my brother. Watching George come unglued on a Sunday morning was like sitting next to a silent church fart—it happened in an instant, took you by surprise, and was absurdly funny, but you knew you weren't supposed to laugh. With the sometime exception of the word *shit*—because Terry liked it—profanity was strictly off-limits in our house, especially when it involved God damning a person, place, or thing. I squirmed under the knowledge that when Terry found out, my father would surely be in big trouble.

George dropped his knife and bounced toward us, his chef T-shirt snaps ready to let go and his rolled-up pants swinging loosely around his broomstick legs. He wiped his bloody hands on a bar towel and tossed it over his shoulder. His hair stretched high in every direction, like he had just escaped the asylum. "You're late, mister." Mister was Lady Jane's male counterpart. Mister showed up when there was no gas left in George's car. "And have you ever heard of a razor? You can march right back down those stairs, go home, and shave." Then he looked at his watch and said, "You have ten minutes."

Of course, Jeremiah marched right back down those stairs, went home, shaved, dragged himself back, changed into his chef clothes, and set about his weekly task of setting up the brunch.

It was a big job, setting up the brunch. A million little pieces had to be put in place before 10 a.m., and almost everything involved a trip down the stairs and into the back of the basement, approximately a half mile away from where we served. Jeremiah had to park the eighteen-wheeler and fill it with water; arrange the pancake griddle; set up the omelet station; and make sure there were spoons, forks, tongs, ladles, spatulas, portable ovens, fuel, buckets, sauté pans, plates, props, and towels. He had to make sure serving tables were skirted, electrical cords were covered by duct tape, and ice was crushed—and then there was the food. The eighteen-wheeler had to be filled with scrambled eggs, bacon, sausage, whitefish, veggies, and potatoes. He had to get the pancake batter, set up juices; put out the cold salads, the smoked fish, and the fruit; and place a hundred different omelet fixings just right so they could be reached with speed and accuracy.

And after everything was in its place, he had to put on his happy face and actually make omelets, each one perfect and fluffy, for a million hungry customers. While he did all this, I peeled shrimp and made pancakes. Of course, I wanted his job—not because I thought it was better or easier, but because it was his.

Even on a good day, when his brain was firing on all cylinders, Jeremiah occasionally became mesmerized by the minutiae of the job, wasting precious minutes searching for the perfect sauté pan, the one he had used the week before, the only one in a sea of sauté pans that let him flip an omelet effortlessly. Today it was a ladle. Somewhere, underneath ten thousand miscellaneous utensils, in the bottom of a clear plastic Lexan tub under the counter at the end of the dishwasher, there was a lone one-ounce ladle that measured the precise amount of vegetable oil needed to produce the perfect omelet.

"Goddamn it, Jeremiah, what are you doing? What are you *doing?*" George said, when he found Jeremiah on his knees shaking through a noisy, twisted mass of bigger ladles, tongs, scoops, and balloon whisks, paralyzed by the need to find that one thing and unable to force his foggy brain out of its trance.

"I'm looking for that one ladle."

"There's a hundred ladles right in front of your face. It's nine thirty, there's nothing set up out there, let's go, let's go!" He reached down and pulled up a giant soup ladle. "Look! Here! If it was a snake it would have bit you."

For some reason, sometimes because it was Sunday and he was hungover, but mostly because he was sixteen, Jeremiah had absolutely no sense of urgency. No matter what, he remained unfazed. The brunch had a heartbeat that galloped from the moment my father crossed the threshold of the back door. The whole place throbbed along with the vein in his forehead. Even I could sense it. The key to keeping the pace and not getting trampled was simple: look painfully hassled.

This, thank God, came quickly and naturally to me. I peeled shrimp and cleaned strawberries with the intensity of a brain surgeon. I learned how to speak loudly using laconic phrases. It didn't matter if the person I was speaking to was a mere three feet away. It didn't matter if he or she understood a word I said. The only thing that mattered was that he or she realized how insanely difficult and important my trip to the bathroom was. And I learned how to deliver food to the eighteen-wheeler as if I were delivering an artificial heart.

Jeremiah, on the other hand, meandered around the building, distracted by everything in his path like a second grader walking home from school. And because George found a way to stumble upon every distraction, the nickname "Goddamn It Jeremiah" was born. Everyone used it: the cooks, the bartenders, the waitstaff, even me.

The Packers games were the biggest distraction of all. We all worshiped at the altar of the beloved and detested 1970s and '80s Green Bay Packers football teams. Miraculously, Jeremiah and I managed to do this without fighting. Misery, even among a bitter sibling rivalry (and perhaps even more so) loved company. There'd been but two winning seasons in twenty years, my friends, yet we anxiously awaited each and every kickoff like kids awaited Christmas morning. But for us Santa never came; instead, we received the likes of Dan Devine, Forrest Gregg, and Lindy Infante. Each week, though, depending on the hang time of the kickoff, gave us a brief moment of hope.

At twelve thirty, the spirit of Curly Lambeau called and Jeremiah walked to the bar. There was nothing covert about his movements. He just checked his watch, set his spatula down, turned off his ovens, slipped right past George who was playing cat and mouse with a pile of sausages, and headed for the TV. I watched in awe and disbelief. There were no customers in line, but still, leaving his spot at the omelet station in the middle of brunch took some serious balls.

It took George about sixty seconds to notice. Brandishing his tongs, he turned and skipped around the wall toward the bar. I followed. The snap of his heels and the *click* of his tongs produced a lyrical echo across the ceiling of the rotunda as he advanced across the warped hardwood floor. Jeremiah sat on the edge of the banquette, facing the screen, with his ankles and arms crossed, just as if he were sitting on the floor of our living room. Even with George bearing down on him, he didn't move an inch. I half expected my dad to pile drive him into the red vinyl.

Instead, he stopped short, sucked in a quick breath between his gritted teeth, and whispered with a twitch, *"Goddamn it,* Jeremiah."

Then Dad paused, looked up, and asked, "What's the score?"

7

Mother's Day

I was still a beginner when I worked my first Mother's Day brunch, too stupid to be afraid. My father and I drove in from the lake, the same as we had for almost a year, except we started out an hour early. He was unusually quiet and über-twitchy that morning. As we were leaving the house, Terry, wearing a relaxed smile and a seersucker bathrobe, sank into the corner of the couch with the Sunday crossword puzzle and a pen. She never looked up when she lit her cigarette and said, "Bye-bye."

In the Pandl household, Mother's Day wasn't about our mother at all—it was about everybody else's mother. It looks a little sad from where I sit now, but that's just the way it worked. We rarely celebrated the day, and we never went out. The mere suggestion of going to a restaurant on Mother's Day, even if we didn't have to work, was considered blasphemous. We knew better. We stayed home, or we worked, in the thick of things for sure, but always carefully existing on the fringe of Mother's Day, sidestepping the bulge and crush of the raggedy-ass greeting-card masses.

So Terry's reality, every Mother's Day, was solitude. I couldn't say with absolute certainty whether or not she liked it, but somehow I sensed she did. Hell, after thirty-odd years of listening to us needle each other to the edge of insanity; years of screaming, yelling, pinching, scratching, pulling hair, and slamming doors; of waiting for small change, nuts, bolts, Barbie shoes, and army men to show up in somebody's poop, who wouldn't embrace a little alone time?

George drove in silence with one hand on the wheel while he chewed the fingernails off the other and spit them on my side of the dashboard. It was like I wasn't even there. Actually, it was like *he* wasn't even there. We did not play the "what are you thinking?" game, nor did we play the "guess the time on the bank clock" game. Instead, he held the windshield in such an intense, trancelike stare, I found myself leaning over and looking for cracks, or bugs, or a spinning sun.

When we finally pulled into the parking lot, he let out a gigantic sigh of resignation and said, "Here we go," as if we were lining up for a firing squad.

My first task of the day was to slice smoked turkey. The brunch had silver platters of smoked turkey, arranged in neat piles around the rim, with a dish of Durkee's mustard in the center. Anything smoked, according to my undeveloped palate, was disgusting, but I knew better than to complain. Miss Willie handed me a gray bus tub loaded with medium-sized turkey breasts and, in what seemed like slow motion, pointed to the slicer.

As a rule, I was unafraid of inanimate objects, but I had seen enough horror movies to know that you had to watch yourself around garbage disposals, lawn mowers, and meat slicers. In my imagination, the meat slicer watched me, with eyes and teeth like Cujo's. There were times when I'd step around it, pressing myself up against the wall in order to avoid falling prey to its razor-sharp circular blade. Worse, George knew the carnage it was capable of, yet he treated the thing as if it belonged in the Smithsonian. "You have to take it apart and clean it *every* time!" he'd yell. "Like this." Then he would gently dismantle its pieces, polish them until he could see his reflection, put them together again, stand back, and admire its beauty. "Like that," he'd say with a slightly demonic smile.

A few years earlier, I had seen the slicer try to eat my sister Peggy. That day, someone must have brought me along for the ride and then decided to put me to work. I stood a few feet away, peeling potatoes. Peggy was slicing green peppers in swift, rhythmic strokes. Just as I was admiring her command of the great stainless beast, I saw a fat bubble of blood squirt off the blade and splatter as it hit the wall.

"Shit," she said quietly, pulling her hand away and wrapping it in her apron.

I ran over and said, "Lemme see."

Blood poured down the back of her hand and clung to the soft hair on her arm as she peeled away the apron. She held up her index finger and gave it a tentative bend.

"What is that?" I asked, watching two folds of skin open up around her knuckle and reveal a thick slice of something grotesquely white.

She lifted her finger to get a better look. "I think it's my bone."

I bent over, put my left hand on my knee, and dry-heaved into my right. The black rubber floor mat spun like it was circling a drain. "You better show Dad."

So she did. At the restaurant, however, his sympathy was infinitesimal. He just shook his head and said, "Sorry, but there's no one to cover your shift. You're gonna have to stay and get it stitched up after lunch."

"Really? You're kidding, right?" she asked.

"No, I'm not. Just wrap it up and put a couple gloves on."

So she did.

I know for a fact that these days it's against the law to let a thirteen-year-old operate a meat slicer. Perhaps it was the law even back then, but those rules never applied to us, so on my first Mother's Day brunch I went ahead and got started on the turkey. I worked slowly, carefully drawing the carriage back with the handle of the pusher, sliding it forward and slipping even peels of turkey into the palm of my hand, never taking my eyes off the spinning blade.

Around me, though, the rest of the world had been set in fast-forward. It was not a normal Sunday. Oven doors slammed. Bacon sizzled. Eggs cracked. Serrated stainless-steel teeth chewed through pineapple, watermelon, and cantaloupe rinds. And all the while the air gathered in a nervous curl of energy, like the sky turning yellow, or like the ocean receding in advance of a tsunami.

The kitchen smelled the same, like every other Sunday morning, but I knew something was different when Miss Willie sidled up to me and whispered in my ear, "Girrrrl, your daddy wants you to run the brunch." There was a scary little laugh buried deep in her chestnut eyes.

"What's so funny?"

"Oh, you'll see. You'll see."

"What?"

"Uh-uh . . . nooo," she said. She shook her head, still giggling as she walked away.

Miss Willie had worked there since before I was born. She commanded a frightening reverence, and my father had made her word the law. The last thing you needed was Willie criticizing your work or your speed. God help me, I could never keep up with her. Hard-boiled eggs, shrimp, kiwi—when it came to peeling, she bested me at least two dozen to one. She peeled cantaloupe like an apple, with a ten-inch serrated knife curled in her fingers. It was downright heroic. She always looked a little war torn: crooked bandanna, burned apron, and frayed and dirty shirt, like she had just battled a bazooka loaded with pancake batter. Her arms were covered in a smattering of caramel-colored scars, some stringy and thin, some bulbous and thick, from years of brushing up against the doors of the convection oven.

Miss Willie ran the salad department. She had two favorites in my family, Chrissy and Amy, and every one of us knew it. She told them all her secrets, shared her baking tricks, including every single ingredient. With the rest of us, she'd wait until our backs were turned and then toss something into the mix, something that made her chocolate mousse pie and her schaum tortes stand in perfect peaks, while ours were limp and watery. I felt bad about it for a while, thinking she didn't like me, but then I learned that she did this to the local newspaper too. From time to time her recipes were printed there, but she always left something out: a spin, a fold, a pinch. The next day dozens of frustrated customers called, wondering why their banana cream pie neither looked nor tasted like the one they had eaten at Pandl's.

A few minutes later, Katie came around. "You better make sure everything's full out there today," she said, with unusual intensity. Her eyes were wide, her brows taut. "I'm not kidding. No screwing around today or Dad'll drop his basket."

"Okay."

"Just make sure nothing gets less than half full. Okay?"

"Okay." I rolled my eyes. As if I didn't know. Jeez.

The restaurant doors opened at nine, an hour earlier than usual. Within minutes, the dining room was stuffed with mothers and their children. Bodies zipped in and around the tables, galloping toward the buffet, keeping a freakish high-frequency *William Tell* overture-like time. Had I been witnessing it from afar, or on TV, perhaps it would have seemed amazing, even amusing, but being there was actually quite frightening. I worried that I might get trampled and end up suffocating under a twisted pile of panty hose and pink sweaters sets from Chadwicks of Boston. My first instinct was to run for my life, but I knew that was out of the question at this point, so I ran around in circles ten thousand, maybe twenty thousand times, going from the dining room to the kitchen and back again. The kitchen was noisy with the percussion of banging plates, clanging glassware, sliding sheet pans, pouring juice, and scraping knives. Everyone knew what to do and nobody talked. The dining room was the exact opposite—everyone talked and no one knew what to do.

Serving was a two-man job, divided unevenly between George and Katie. They stood side by side. He served the whitefish and the vegetable—that day it was green beans—and Katie served everything else: scrambled eggs, sausage, bacon, and American fried potatoes. The whitefish was delicate and therefore more time consuming.

"How about a beautiful tail?" I heard him ask somebody's mom. "No bones in the tail."

"Sure."

My father slid the tail next to her scrambled eggs like it was a recently dusted artifact prepared for carbon dating.

"Isn't that just gorgeous?" he said. "It's *gorgeous,* isn't it?" Twitch. "Almost too pretty to eat." Twitch. Laugh.

The mom gave him a tense smile and a nod and moved on. Customers gave him that look on Sundays all the time—bewildered, sympathetic, yet scared.

As I ran back to the kitchen to retrieve a fresh

stack of hot plates, I was stopped by one of the waiters, Larry Miller. Larry was a younger guy, but he had worked there for quite a while, long enough to appreciate, and respect, the fact that George's little idiosyncrasies grew exponentially along with the number of reservations in the book.

"Psst, Julie," he whispered, and waved me over toward the coffeemakers. "Come here."

I smiled and peeked under the mammoth urns. "You got some bacon hidden under there?"

"No." He laughed.

A few weeks earlier, my father had come around the corner just in time to see Larry about to shove a couple of pieces of bacon in his mouth, so he had ditched them under the big urns, hoping George wouldn't notice. But George did, of course, and coughed up a frenzied lecture on the evils of wastefulness, ending with, "WOULD YOU THROW BACON AROUND LIKE THAT IN YOUR HOUSE?"

"See that kid over there?" Larry pointed to a little busboy with curly blond hair, standing in front of the dish machine, dividing piles of flatware into bus bins. His black pants were sucked in tightly between his pudgy butt cheeks.

"Yeah."

"He's new."

"He's new, brand new, like today's his first day?"

"Yep."

"Poor guy." Honestly, despite the fact that he was at least three years older than me, I wanted to cry for the kid.

"He just came up to me and asked, 'Who's that big fat guy running around yelling at everyone?'"

Larry and I stood there, both of us clutching the drain under the coffee spigots, doubled over laughing.

"What did you tell him?"

"I said, 'Ah, that big fat guy is Mr. Pandl, and he's the one who signs your paycheck.' Then he asked me not to tell."

It happened all the time. Kids slid through the interview process because they owned a pair of black pants and could breathe. They arrived at work their first day thinking, *Easy cash, how hard can it be to bus tables?*

Then they ran into George. He worked alongside everyone else, so it was easy to mistake him for a line cook or a dishwasher. There was no formal let's-do-lunch introduction. Instead, my father would do things like toss a five-dollar bill underneath a pile of lettuce he'd found lying on the floor outside the second walk-in and watch bus kids walk back and forth, lugging bundles of tablecloths and napkins up the stairs, stepping over, and sometimes directly on, the greens. He waited, busying himself, counting the number of

113

times each person ignored the mess until his level of frustration threatened to produce cardiac arrest, and then he stopped the unlucky new kid, grabbing him or her by the arm. Lifting the lettuce leaves and pointing to the cash, he then exclaimed, "Look here!"

"Cool," was the standard response. Easy cash, right?

"COOL? COOL? Who do you think put that there, Santa Claus?"

"Umm . . ."

"Do you know how many times you walked over this lettuce? *Do you?*"

"No."

"Eighteen! Eighteen times. You'd be rich right now if you had bothered to bend over and clean it up. Right?"

"I guess."

"Well, now you know. Next time, when you see a mess, clean it up." Then he'd pick up the money, slip it back in his wallet, and walk away. Not exactly your standard welcome aboard, but it made an impression.

Still laughing and wiping tears from my eyes, I went behind the dish machine to grab the plates. The machine belched heavy clouds of steam as it pushed the plates, lined up in plastic racks like soldiers marching into battle, toward the end of the conveyor. Each plate was delivered from the mouth of the dragon at a temperature of something like twenty thousand degrees. I held my breath and pulled them, two by two, and placed them in stacks where the racks stopped, wondering if the water temperature was hot enough to evaporate my fingerprints forever. When the stacks grew tall enough, I leaned a pile carefully against my chest, turned toward the dining room, and whimpered. Waiting for them to cool down was out of the question. Hot plates were literally a physical necessity when it came to keeping order in George's world. Delivering cold plates might have been on par with strutting into the dining room naked, stopping at a table, and taking a bite out of somebody's pancakes.

I looked like an orangutan dragging a bowling ball by the time I made it out to the buffet, knees buckling and wobbly, knuckles sweeping along the carpeting, and face with a primatelike scowl. Naturally, a long line had formed.

I cursed Hallmark.

I cursed Mother's Day.

I cursed everything that went with it—the cards, the stores, the tchotchke stationery, the keepsake ornaments, and the Hall of Fame movies.

The edges of the plates burned corduroy stripes into my forearms while pellets of sweat poured over my temples. I squatted down to give myself some leverage and heaved the swaying stack under the heat lamp.

Just then, I heard my father stutter, "Get me . . .

get . . . me . . . get me . . . the beans . . . the . . . beans without skin . . . skin." I didn't have to look. I could see by the way the customers gawked that his words were accompanied by a series of twitches and spasms. They all looked at me as if to say, "Does he need to be medicated or confined?" One woman in particular locked eyes with me for a split second; hers were cold and brilliantly blue, but her expression was soft. She was somebody's mother. Somebody had picked the place, made the plans, and brought her there. She was celebrating.

I knew what he meant. He needed more of the American fried potatoes, *without* skin. The green beans—*with* skin, of course—sat right next to the potatoes in the steam table. The crowd caused the two to become one in George's mind. I understood, and I hoped she did too.

I held her gaze and smiled. "I got it, Dad," I said. "I'll be right back."

8

·————

Rise and Shine

In my memory, some days stick out like a sore thumb, others like an ax in the forehead. When my sister Katie turned thirty, I was sixteen. She had the unfortunate luck of being born on New

Year's Eve, a nice tax deduction for Terry and George, but her thunder was often dulled by the aftereffects of Christmas, or stolen altogether by the fact that it was a new year for everybody. For her thirtieth birthday, our friend Meg planned a surprise party at Echo Bowl for a date three weeks after the fact in January, hoping to throw Katie off the scent. Echo Bowl—a bowling alley–cum–tavern–cum–video arcade—wasn't exactly "dinner at the Ritz," but the place was as much a part of the landscape of our lives as it was a part of the landscape of Milwaukee, so it fit the bill.

Because George and I were slated to work the brunch the next day, he and Terry and I had to hit four thirty Mass at St. Eugene's that Saturday, and then head down Port Road to the bowling alley. Four thirty Mass, no matter where, was a little like a sedative for my father. The second reading pulled him under like clockwork. I sat between him and my mother and drove my elbow into his ribs whenever he drifted into a snore.

"I'm thinking," he said, his eyelids popping open as if he really were just thinking.

"You're snoring," I whispered.

"Really," he said, in feigned surprise.

"Yeah, really."

We arrived at Echo Bowl around six. From the outside, the place reminded me a little of the restaurant, but the settings were decidedly

117

different. Pandl's neighborhood was serene and orderly, whereas noisy fast-food chains and splashy car dealerships flanked Echo Bowl. Both buildings, however, had a crudely out-of-place steel arch that stretched like a sooty rainbow from one end to the other, leftovers from a puzzling architectural fad. The similarities ended there, though, thank God. Echo Bowl had a stale smell that burrowed into your jacket, your sweater, your jeans, and your hair. It stuck with you for days, like someone had stuffed a pack of beer-battered and deep-fried Pall Malls in your pocket or under your pillow.

I steered my mother toward the stairs leading down to the private party room in the basement, past the bar, the shoe rental desk, and the arcade, while my father sauntered behind, soaking it all in. He had a silly smirk on his face and a twinkle in his eye. He wasn't a bowler—at least I'd never seen him do it—but something about the atmosphere appealed to him. Happy chatter cut through thick smoke in the bar, while beer from taps flowed steadily into eight-ounce pilsners. Rubber-soled red and white shoes—circle heel-stamps bearing the sizes—soft and moist from collective use, slipped back and forth across the Formica countertop in one queer yet welcome exchange after another. A symphony of jingles, blips, clanks, and twitters, along with a torrent of electric blue light, burst from the arcade. And underneath it all was the slow rumble of hard resin rolling down slick maple. The noisy, uncomplicated energy tickled my father's twitch. He had a way of enjoying things exactly as they were. He loved local color, even if it came with carpeting that smelled like a St. Bernard that had been bathed in Budweiser.

Katie got wise when her friends directed her down the basement stairs, but her face lit up with surprise nonetheless. Parties have a way of folding into each other over time. After a while, they all start to look the same—bunches of primary-colored balloons tied to sandbags in the center of paper tablecloths, a stray one floating here and there against a dropped ceiling; clear plastic cups filled with too much foam; gag gifts about being over the hill; a box of Depend; a pair of big beige granny panties, and a flurry of familiar faces all add up to thirty, or forty, and maybe fifty. When the gag gifts become functional, the parties take on a different shape.

Katie's party was no different, except that I was finally old enough to mingle with the adults. And because my parents were present, I was able to drink beer. The rules regarding drinking in our family were designed to establish what you might call a relaxed responsibility. Granted, the design had some serious flaws—nine of them, to be exact—but the intent, I believe, was earnest. When we were booster-seat small, my father served us tiny chasers of beer with dinners that included sauerkraut or red cabbage, stating that it was downright criminal to drink milk with such foods. As we grew older, we were allowed to have an occasional beer at family functions or while kibitzing around the kitchen table. Beer, incidentally, was okay; everything else was not. Supervision was the key, but by the time I came along, the lock had been picked a thousand times.

I had my first full beer on a crisp September day in a bar in Munich when I was fourteen, a freshman in high school. A bunch of us had traveled to Germany, Austria, and Switzerland with a group from the Wisconsin Restaurant Association. George ordered the beer for me. The server, who looked like she had just jumped off a bottle of St. Pauli Girl, dropped four gigantic steins of Paulaner Dunkel in the center of the table: one for George, one for Stevie, one for Amy, and one for me. With a practiced flick of his wrist, my father slid mine over through the splash of beer the waitress had left behind. My eyes bulged. "Dad, this is as big as my head," I said. "There's no way I can drink all this."

He smiled and said, "Just finish what you can," and sank his upper lip into a thick white peak. He closed his eyes, took three long gulps, and pulled the stein away. "Ahh, it's like coming home," he declared, before licking the suds off his whiskers. His appreciation had always made beer look as if it could cure cancer, but that day it seemed heightened by the fact that he was sharing it among his people, past and present. Even I could sense that on this occasion it was more than just a beer. It was a slightly bitter but warm and malty rite of passage.

The biggest flaw of my father's relaxed-responsibility plan may have been me. By age sixteen I was, by definition, naughty and sneaky in an overt way unique to babies of the family. At Katie's party I made fast friends with the bartender and proceeded to consume cup after cup of keg beer. Katie's friends welcomed me into their conversations, and I managed to hold up my end, wandering in and out of duos and threesomes like a pro, sampling hors d'oeuvres and offering to run for drinks. Around nine George tapped me on the shoulder and said, "We're leaving."

"Can I stay?"

"Go ask the boss," he said, deferring to Mom.

My mother sat at a table nearby, chatting with Jeremiah. I slid next to them and asked her if I could stay.

"I don't think so, honey. You've got to work tomorrow, and how are you going to get out to the lake?"

"Please, Mom," I pleaded.

Jeremiah interjected and gestured with his cup, "Just let her stay, Mom. I'm going out there tonight. She can come with me."

She put her hand on his arm, looked him in the eye, and said, "This is your baby sister."

"Mom, it's fine. She'll be fine. Don't worry about it."

"All right, but don't be too late."

IT WAS MIDNIGHT before our shoes crunched on the ice and snow as we made our way across the parking lot to Jeremiah's light blue Omni. "You wanna go out?" he asked over the hood of the car.

"Where?" I asked, dropping like a rag doll into the frozen bucket seat and rubbing my mittens together.

"To a bar."

"Jere, I can't get into a bar." My breath produced a cloud that settled into the windshield.

"This bar you can get into. Trust me."

Excited to be both under his wing and at his side, I trusted. We went to a bar called Smitty's on Keefe Avenue, just off Humboldt. At the time it was a dicey neighborhood—not necessarily rape-and-murder dicey but not a bad place to buy a dime bag through the tinted window of a Gran Torino either. Had she known where he was taking me, Terry would have hit the roof. In the eighties, people went down there for two reasons: one, the bars tended to overlook underage drinking; two, Albanese's, a tiny hole-in-the-wall on Keefe, had a garlic spinach pasta so good it was truly worth getting shot at.

Honestly, I was cooked the minute he pulled the car out of the bowling alley parking lot. The quick right turn, the spring of the clutch, and the other cars moving in the opposite direction on Port Road all provided an undetected bit of foreshadowing and made my eyeballs turn in on my stomach. I felt a flash of pain and a mozzarella stick tried to throw itself up, but I locked my jaw around it and swallowed hard, determined not to wimp out on Jeremiah.

I opened the car door into a dirty snowbank, stumbled over it, and followed him into Smitty's. A heavy cloud of smoke settled in and around piles of crisply permed hair. The place was January—humid, a mixture of sweaty wool, bad breath, stale beer, and ancient radiators. I leaned into a bar stool draped with an abandoned black peacoat and a red wool scarf; its tassels lying in the gray slush on the floor.

"Two Miller Lites, tap," Jeremiah shouted over the dizzying whoosh of voices muddled with music.

The bartender, John, was a friend of his. John wiped his hands on a clean white towel, slung it over his shoulder, looked over at me, smiled, and said, "How old's your friend?"

123

Jeremiah smiled back. "This is my sister. She's twenty-two."

It was one of those moments, the kind where you realize you're past the point of no return. The room seesawed and I knew I was in trouble. Jeremiah handed me my beer and said, "Are you okay?"

"Yeah, I'm fine." I hiccuped.

"Sure?"

"Yep."

"Okay." He turned around and headed toward a group of his friends seated at a table against the wall.

I poked him in the back with my mitten and said, "I'll be right back." Hiccup.

"Okay. I'll be with these guys." He gestured to a blur of pasty white Wisconsin winter faces.

I side-winded my way toward the back of the bar, figuring there had to be a bathroom back there somewhere. I set my glass down next to a girl with too much black eyeliner and wearing gold earrings the size of salad plates, each of which offered a nauseatingly distorted reflection of my head, like I was looking at it in the side of a car door. I backed away, wobbled into the ladies' room, and latched the door.

Options tend to narrow at an alarming rate when you're on the verge of throwing up. You have just a few terrifying seconds to look around and make choices about where you will and where you will not put your head and hands. Throwing up meant defeat; it meant that I could not keep up, what felt, at the time, like a fate worse than death, so I chose to lie on the floor, sandwiched between the toilet and the wall, with my cheek against the cold, wet tile and the bottoms of my Tretorns against the door. I'll admit, not exactly an Audrey Hepburn moment, but what are you gonna do? A dark, rippled water line separated the top and bottom halves of the wood molding at the base of the wall. I found a soothing rhythm, breathing in and out over each tiny wave, broken every ten seconds by the rattle of the door against my heels. Finally, a loud voice from the other side cried, "What the fuck's going on in there? C'mon, I gotta pee!"

Worried about embarrassing—or worse, disappointing—my brother, I made a move to stand. I raised myself to my knees and rested my arms and head on the toilet seat. My shadow hovered for a few seconds in the tea-colored water, undulating along with the music. In one rubbery motion, I grabbed the seat with my mittens, pushed up, turned around, and undid the latch. Earring girl got tangled up in her white leather pirate boots and fell past me as I swung open the door. "Bitch," she said, falling into the wall. I tried to see my reflection in her earrings. It crossed my mind to point to them and ask if her pimp knew that she had stolen his hubcaps, but instead I just made a beeline for the front door and stumbled to the car.

Within a few minutes, Jeremiah knocked on the passenger's-side window. "What're you doing?"

"Closing my eyes."

"You can't just leave without telling me. I didn't know where the hell you were."

"Sorry."

"Are you sick?"

"Uh-huh."

"Why didn't you say something?"

"I didn't want you to be mad."

"I'm not mad. Jesus! Just don't leave like that. We can go home."

" 'Kay."

THE NEXT MORNING, the sound of my father's voice was like a bag of goldfish swimming in my head. "Rise and shine," he sang. "Daylight in the swamps." His words made my brain wobble and threw me off balance, despite the fact that I remained motionless, frozen in the fetal position, like a dead person, wrapped in thick flannel sheets, waiting to be tossed into the trunk of a car.

"C'mon, time to get up."

My eyeballs declared themselves painfully present within their throbbing orbs. I felt my eyelids separate and peel themselves slowly in the opposite direction over thick, buttery mucus.

"I'm up," I said, putting the screws to my gray matter.

"We're already running late. You've got twenty minutes."

" 'Kay."

I heard his slippers sliding up the slate stairs in the foyer, and I closed my eyes. I had a feeling that just standing up was going to be a problem. The thought of working an entire brunch forced my dehydrated body to produce a couple of small, miraculous tears. As they squeezed themselves out of the corners of my eyes and slipped onto the sheets, I wondered if the day would actually kill me. Death was certainly near. I could smell him in the room; he hovered around my head, his presence a greasy cheeseburger served in a dirty shoe store ashtray. I thought perhaps it was just my breath until I sat up and he dropped his scythe cleanly down the center of my skull. If not for the fact that my skin was pulled tightly around my head, so much so that it made my hair hurt, I believe my cranium would have split into two neatly symmetrical bowls. I clutched two fistfuls of flannel, waiting for the shock to wear off or sink in, waiting for the room to right itself.

"Hey, get up!" Jeremiah shouted.

He stood still, but as I looked over, his body seemed to splash about the doorjamb like a rubber duck.

"I'm sick," I said.

"No kidding."

"No, Jere, I'm like, hospital sick."

He laughed.

"I'm not kidding. I'm not gonna make it."

"Too bad."

"I can't. I swear."

"You know what Dad'll say."

"What?" I asked rhetorically, knowing that suffering was my only way through, knowing that the path back to bed ran directly through the brunch, no detours and no excuses.

" 'You gotta pay to play, baby.' You better get movin'. I'm leaving. You're riding with Dad."

"No, I can't. You have to wait for me. You have to . . ."

He was already gone, up the stairs and out the door. His car started with a rumble I hadn't noticed the night before. I heard him grind it into reverse and back out onto the gravel road.

I stood up and bounced from the closet door to the footboard to the dresser to the doorjamb to the wall and to the other wall until I reached the bathroom. I filled my trembling hands with cold water, splashed it on my face, and looked in the mirror. I expected to see a carcass on my shoulders, bulging rigor mortis remains, some-thing akin to roadkill, but I looked pretty good. I was amazed at how I could feel so utterly exoskeletal, yet appear so . . . well, normal.

Aside from the waxy grayish pallor of my cheeks, the rheumy pileup around my eyes, and the angora sweaters on my teeth, I looked like I did every other Sunday morning.

The ride to the restaurant was marked by a searing pain that came on the heels of opening my eyes. The sun shone brightly that morning; it bounced violently off the snow-covered cornfields and sent unyielding, searing rays of reflective light directly into my irises. My father, chipper as usual, talked, but about what I have no idea. The words disassembled themselves upon exiting his lips—they didn't line up like they were supposed to. Instead, they formed an angry mob, wielding baseball bats, brass knuckles, and rubber hoses inside my brain, quieted only by the brace of the icy window against my forehead.

MY FATHER CONFIRMED the fact that he was on to me when he dropped a box of smoked trout next to my cutting board, said, "Set these up," and laughed.

One of my co-workers, a kid named Jeff, was peeling pineapple on a board a few feet away.

"Very funny," I said, gagging.

George's shoulders shook as he walked away. I had shown weakness a few months before, complaining about how disgusting this task was, when Amy had originally taught me how to do it.

Dad knew that even on a good day, cleaning trout made my stomach turn, and this was not a good day. I had no one to blame but myself.

Jeff looked over, took pity on me, and said, "I'll do 'em if you want. I'm almost done with these." It's what we did, watched each other's backs. I was the boss's kid, sure, but it didn't take long for all of us to unite as a defense around George's Sunday weirdness.

"No, thanks," I said, knowing that the assignment was a punishment, effective and efficient, and any attempt at worming my way out of it would be met with the dreaded "Dad disappointment."

Breathing through my mouth, I pulled off the waxy box top and peeled back a shroud of baking paper flecked with bits of brown gelatinous goo. They were dead, all right, good and smoked, laid out in three neat rows, but there was something strangely alert in their lifeless eyes, like they were just an impossible blink away from shouting, "Ha, ha, you have to work the brunch." I picked one up between my thumb and forefinger and dropped it on my cutting board. "You stink. You know that?" I said. It stared blankly at me, like fish do, dead or alive. "And you're stupid too."

I grabbed a boning knife, slipped it above the gills, pressed down until I felt a spine, twisted, and slid it down the length to the tail. The sensation, and the noise the blade made, snapping through tiny bones like teeth on a comb, made me shiver. I could handle a chicken breast or a tenderloin just fine, but I never liked having the whole structure of a thing—its lifeless, breathless shape—under my knife. There was something too immediate, too apparent about its pre-edible existence. It's not that I felt sorry for it; no, I could not have cared less about the fish. I felt sorry for myself, for having such an unsympathetic father who made me perform such atrocities, ignoring my weakened condition.

I set the first side on a tray next to my board, cut off the head and tail, and went to work peeling the spinal column from the second side. The trick was to pull the spine out in one piece, which meant less digging for errant bones. It came out clean. I was feeling around for pinbones when George came back and spotted the lonely head sitting off to the side. "Don't forget the cheeks."

"God, Dad, I know, I got it, all right?" I snapped.

"Don't throw those away. They're the best part, you know," he said happily.

"I *know*." If there was a part, a disgusting part that no one else—no sane person anyway— would dare eat, my dad inevitably declared it "the best part." I think it was a Depression trick.

I swear to God, if he saw you throwing away the crusty anus off a roasted duck, he'd swat your hand away and say, "Hey, hey, *hey,* what're you *doing?* That's the best part!"

Before I had the chance, he grabbed the fish head, poked his index finger into its cheek, pulled out a slab of smoky flesh, and stuck it in his mouth. "Delicious. Here," he said, and waved a piece under my nose. "Try some."

"Dad, c'mon," I pleaded, putting my hand up and backing away.

"All right. You don't know what you're missing, though," he said as he left.

It was the half-eaten head that finally did it. I couldn't resist the urge to look at it. Like standing on the edge of a cliff and feeling compelled to jump off, I stared. There it was, just a severed head, a dark tea-colored shadow of itself, gaunt and bodiless, staring back at me through a hazy membrane that covered the rubbery eyeballs. I brought a shaky hand up to my mouth.

"Are you okay?" Jeff asked.

"I'll be right back." I turned and ran for the bathroom, where Katie's thirtieth birthday finally exacted its hefty price. It equaled twenty minutes of ribs and diaphragm colliding, in attempt after excruciating attempt to break free from my torso. When I came back, each fish was laid neatly on a bed of leaf lettuce, halves side by side, with lemon slices, parsley sprigs, and queen olives instead of heads. They actually looked . . . sort of . . . appetizing.

I HAD SWEAT out the nausea during my job of running the brunch, but blood continued to stretch my temples tight, making them throb. I gripped the steering wheel as we headed home.

"Jeff asked me for a raise today," George said, looking at the paper.

Why my father decided to share this information with me, crippled as I was with consequences, I can't say. It was odd, though. We never discussed pay rates—not even mine— before or after that day. Decisions like that belonged to him and him alone. After all, at sixteen, what did I know?

"What'd you say?"

"I said I'd take it up with the board." He smiled.

Probably because I had spent the entire brunch hovering between life and death, I had a minor epiphany. Turned out, I did know something. I worked in the middle, in that place where my co-workers, who had become friends, met my father. Crazy, absolutely, but I could not have them thinking he was unfair. I looked over at him with my hands on the wheel.

"Dad, that is soooo mean."

"What? Why?" He laughed.

"There is no board, Dad. You're the board. *God,* I can't believe how *mean* you are."

"Well, I told him the board would consider it."

"Dad, c'mon, you gotta call him tomorrow and tell him he can have it."

"Well . . ." He took a sip of his drink and raised his eyebrow. "It's under consideration." He nodded affirmatively.

His nonchalance pissed me off. I slid a sweaty palm down my cheek. "No, Dad. Do you know how hard it was for him to ask? Give it to him. He works really hard."

"I guess it was."

"I *know* it was, Dad. Just give it to him."

"I'll think about it."

"No, Dad. Tell me you're gonna do it."

He paused for a second, squinted at the car in front of us, and said, "You think so?"

"*Yes!* I think so."

"I think I will, then."

I flipped the blinker right and checked over my shoulder to switch lanes. He turned back to his paper, but I caught him, in the passenger's mirror, just for an instant, smiling a contented grin.

9

Walkin'-around Money

As a kid I had two sources of income: walkin'-around money, which was a gift from my father's wallet, and loose change, which I stole from a box full of quarters hidden on the top shelf in my parents' closet. The notion of receiving an allowance in our house was really just that, a notion. It was talked about, but mine never once materialized; in fact, to save my life, I couldn't tell you what the imaginary dollar amount was. My father supported the idea of an allowance, though, because he needed it in order to champion an elaborate system of fines, established in an effort to teach us that everything, by golly, comes at a price. For instance: if we left the lights on when exiting the family room, he'd say something like, "Do you own stock in the electric company? I'm docking your allowance a nickel." Or if he called the house and I answered the telephone saying just "Hello" instead of "Hello, *Pandl's*," it cost me a nonexistent quarter. Leaving an unfinished can of grape Graf's soda on the coffee table cost an uncollected buck. I have no idea why, but the system seemed to work.

I suppose an allowance of, say, five bucks a week, multiplied by nine and then again by four, would have taken a sizable chunk out of the monthly budget. So instead of adhering to any weekly obligation—outside of his imagination, that is—from time to time, my father reached in his wallet and pulled out what he called "walkin'-around money."

The St. Robert's Fair meant there'd be walkin'-around money for all of us. The fair happened—and continues to happen—on the first weekend in June. I looked forward to it with anxious anticipation that rivaled my birthday and Christmas Eve. The fair marked the end of the school year and was a rare day of absolute freedom. Beginning the summer after second grade, my parents let me fly solo.

I remember those first weeks in June being warmer than they are now, or perhaps I've gone colder with age. I wore a pair of white Izod shorts with green trim, a matching green T-shirt, and a battered pair of PF Flyers. My new bike—a First Holy Communion gift—parted the heat evenly around me. It pulled my hair softly to each side as I rode down Prospect Avenue, cut across Jarvis, and turned the corner onto Farwell. Dozens of wood-paneled station wagons lined the street next to the playground. I pedaled up the curb and onto the sidewalk, tossed my bike in the rack, and went to hunt down my dad.

"He'll be in the book bin!" my mother had shouted as I skipped down the back steps, the screen door slamming behind me. As if I didn't know.

Even at age eight I knew my father's first love was books. Certainly they came before the restaurant, perhaps even ahead of my mother and all of us. Words lined up and found a welcome home in his heart. They formed an easy escape, the same way a fishing pole or a set of golf clubs did for other dads, except the escape they offered him was effortless and ever present. His sport required no tackle and no country club membership, so it spoke to his frugality as well as his soul.

I found him at the back of the playground in the shade near the rectory, browsing among rows and rows of musty castoffs, smiling at the thought of finding a hidden ten-cent treasure. "Dad, can I have some walkin'-around money?" He reached in his wallet without a word, pulled out a five-dollar bill, and pressed it into my sweaty palm.

I bent over, tucked the soft bill carefully in the bottom of my moist shoe, and said, "Thanks, Dad."

"You're welcome," he said, and there it was, the easy smile. It piqued my curiosity, that smile, but its quiet, generous beauty was lost in my impatient desire to get a wagonload of cotton candy evaporating in my cheeks and then bounce around the Moon Walk.

● ● ●

OUTSIDE OF THAT first Sunday in June, I knew better than to ask my parents for money, because as an eight-year-old, what did I need money for? But I needed money, like every other eight-year-old kid in my class, to buy Mike and Ikes, Lemonheads, and Fudgsicles at Hayek's Pharmacy on my way home from school. This is where the box in the closet came in. Having no allowance yet needing to support my growing candy addiction, I quickly resorted to a life of casual crime.

My parents' closet was an L-shaped walk-in and therefore a good hiding place. I spent a lot of time in there, sitting on top of my father's polished wingtip shoes with dry-cleaning bags hanging around my ears. It smelled like Old Spice and Ammens powder, but soapy and feminine too. In springtime, the scent of lilac and magnolia hung in my mother's blouses.

I was five or six when I first laid eyes on the change box, young enough to be excited over the mere sight of it. The box was tall, at least a foot, and square, and was made of clear plastic. Stuck to the rim was a torn remnant of a tag; the other half presumably had been discarded with the lid. The box was full of quarters. Quarters my father retrieved every week from the cigarette machine at the restaurant. I remember thinking, *I can* see *that money up there*. I looked over both shoulders and whispered to no one in particular, "They left it right where I can *see* it." At the time, coins were much more valuable to me than paper money. They weighed more. They could be jingled, stacked, spun, and flipped. And they could be found; on the table next to the washing machine, in between the cushions of the couch, and up there, in a plastic box on the top shelf.

Twice a month I made that climb. The shelves were ill fitting and wobbly, vertical and slippery in my grip and under my socks, yet my fear of dropping backward like a sack of onions onto the hardwood floor was overpowered by my sugar jones. The thought of an endless supply of candy propelled me higher and higher until all I had to do was anchor my feet against the corners, where the shelf met the wall, hold on to the edge of the shelf with the fingers of my left hand, reach over the top of the box with my right, and grab a fistful of cold hard change. It felt fantastic.

For the record, "stealing quarters from the change box in my parents' closet" was written on a tightly folded wad of loose-leaf paper I carried into my first confession—and my second and my third. This sin appeared just above others, like "fighting with my brother" and "not brushing my teeth." I'm a little embarrassed to admit this, but I took advantage of the gift of absolution in a way that I'm pretty sure neither the Catholic church nor the Holy Spirit intended. It wasn't exactly crippling, but the guilt did stick with me for years until I found out that Jeremiah had pinched his fair share of quarters as well. I don't know why, but his admission made the deed seem less like a matter of confession and more like a matter of fact. The good Lord didn't forget, though. My penance arrived just a month or two ago. After polishing off an entire box of Mike and Ikes, something I used to do with ease, I developed a case of heartburn so scorching it had me clutching my chest and contemplating a visit to the emergency room.

As we grew older, walkin'-around money became less of a fiscal anomaly and more of a necessity. See, none of us Pandls got paid for working at the restaurant. There were checks, of course, but we never saw any of the cash. That just wasn't part of the deal, so it never even occurred to me to ask. And even if I had thought of it, I was too afraid to say anything. The money was reserved for college and came with boring lessons regarding financial responsibility. When I was fourteen, my father handed me a paycheck bearing my name—I still remember the amount, $137.17—and told me to go open a checking account. I did. And then I promptly exercised my newfound financial freedom by running to the Id, an aptly named, trendy clothing shop for teenage girls. I picked out a pair of pleated teal pants; a matching blouse with a collar that magically stood "eighties" erect; and a necklace, a gold-beaded, ropy number that hung just below the blouse's second button. It wasn't until after the saleslady took an hour wrapping everything neatly in tissue paper and ringing me up that I realized a library card was an insufficient form of identification. I can't remember how the deal was finished—I believe she had to call the president of the United States—but I do remember leaving with the outfit.

The real lesson came a few weeks later, after my first bank statement arrived. My father balanced his own checkbook to the penny every month, as if he were responsible for the federal budget. Therefore he expected me to do the same. I had written only two checks, one to the Id and one to my mother for "cash." It should have been simple. Instead, it was a process. He slipped his letter opener in the corner of the bank's envelope and slit it along the long edge like he was trimming a tenderloin. He laid the statement on the kitchen table, smoothed it flat, and began sorting the checks and cross-checking them against my register.

"Give me a break," I said, rolling my eyes. "There are only two checks there. Here." I grabbed them and slapped one on top of the other. "One, two."

"Do you want me to show you how to do this?"

"Um . . . not really."

"Well, you're gonna learn, Lady Jane."

In addition to being chewed out for buying something as ridiculous as clothing, the lesson, as I recall, also included a stern scolding about the fact that, as I subtracted, I crossed out the numbers before carrying them. The whole episode left me embarrassed and scarred. I didn't write a check again until I went to college, and I have ten years of unopened bank statements stuffed in shoe boxes in my closet.

There was always a weirdness surrounding money in our house, and as a kid it was confusing as hell. Work hard, and perhaps if you're lucky a few bucks might float your way. Do nothing and the same thing might happen, or not. I imagine other parents had a more consistent approach, but I can see now that my father was not aiming for consistency. Instead, he fired messages from opposite directions, and in the process he somehow managed to eradicate any sense of entitlement on our part. My mother used to call him penny wise and pound foolish. The cliché was true enough, I suppose, but it was like referring to the Sistine Chapel ceiling as a painting, or Shakespeare a writer—the statement lacked the appropriate emotional intensity.

FOR ME THE money messages collided in earnest in 1986, over a can of Planters peanuts at the Drake Hotel in Chicago. I was sixteen.

George and I loaded boxes of books and booze into the back of his pockmarked Subaru station wagon and headed south on a breezy Sunday afternoon in mid-May, with me at the wheel. The National Restaurant Association show was an event we looked forward to with excited anticipation, partly because it was a mecca of learning in my family, but mostly because George reserved rooms at the Drake and took us to five-star restaurants for dinner. Because there were so many of us, we didn't travel much as a family, but the NRA fell into an "educational" category, so if we wanted to, we were all allowed to go. I even got to skip school. The choice was between two days of watching spittle form in the corners of my history teacher's mouth as he droned on about the Civil War versus two days of eating and drinking my way up and down the Magnificent Mile—a no-brainer.

As we merged from the Edens Expressway onto the Kennedy, the Chicago skyline loomed ahead and made me giggle. It was so neatly rigid against the cloudless afternoon sky that it looked a little fake, like a backdrop in a movie. I had a vision of the car ripping through its canvas and splashing into Lake Michigan.

My father leaned over the stick shift and fished his wallet out of his back pocket. "Here," he said, pulling out a hundred-dollar bill and handing it to me. "Here's a little walkin'-around money."

"Thanks, Dad." I folded the bill into a tight square, stuffed it in the pocket of my jeans, and looked over at him. "Thanks. Really."

"You're welcome," he said through an easy smile.

I had grown to appreciate that look on his face as much as I did the cash. His broad grin folded into a wonderfully pink and cheeky hug that wrapped itself around the corners of his eyes. It was a smile I could feel, one that reached out and patted my head. It wasn't about the money. It was generosity equaling appreciation, inching toward something—happiness, I guessed—so quietly beautiful that I couldn't quite put my finger on it.

We arrived in downtown Chicago around five. It had a certain cachet, pulling up to the same simple curb on the Walton side of the Drake that had greeted the likes of Churchill, Garland, DiMaggio, and Sinatra. The glass breezeway, the spit-shined brass buttons on the doorman's coat, the gold-winged dragons with glowing white orbs tucked under the awning—it was all dazzling and elegant. It felt kind of regal, at least for about sixty seconds.

I slid the car into neutral, pulled up the parking brake, and looked over at George. "Well, chief?"

He smiled. "Nice driving."

"Thanks."

"Shall we, madam?" he said, giving a nod to the sophisticated atmosphere.

"But of course," I replied, reaching for the handle on the door. Before I could ease it open myself, a bellhop dressed exactly like a flying monkey from *The Wizard of Oz* heaved it open for me. The driver's-side door had been an issue ever since my sister Peggy had backed into a concrete light assembly in a parking lot and thrown the whole right side out of alignment. The back hatch was tricky to open too. George was famous for not wanting to make a claim to his insurance carrier, though, so more often than not these little imperfections became part of the car's "charm." When the hinge gave a loud pop, the door howled against its jamb, and a dozen or so heads, sitting on top of double-breasted Brooks Brothers flannel and St. John's knits, turned. I realized that we were like the mangy third cousins that show up unannounced for Thanksgiving dinner. I stepped out of the car and gave the bellhop a shrug and a grin.

"Will you be checking in today, ma'am?" he asked, giving a slight bow.

"We will. Thank you."

"Did you need help with your luggage?"

"Please, it's in the back," I said, handing him a five-dollar bill and achieving a slight sense of belonging.

With a twist of his finger, he signaled another bellhop to attend to the luggage. By the time I turned around and reached the back of the car,

George was showing the second guy—Chuck, according to his name tag—how to open the hatch. He set his black wingtip shoe, its seams crusty with Ammens, on the bumper and pressed it down toward the asphalt. "Press down on the hatch . . . like so, and then press the button," he instructed. As the car bounced up, so did the hatch. "Voilà," he said with a little twitch. Honest to God, pulling up in Jed Clampett's jalopy, rocking chair on top and all, would have been just as classy.

I LEANED MY back against the slick beveled-oak edge of the hotel's reservation desk as my father dealt with the check-in.

"We have you booked in one of our corner suites, Mr. Pandl, one queen and two twins. Is that correct?" the woman asked as her fingers clicked around the keyboard.

"That's correct. The rest of us should be here any minute."

Whoever checked in before us had left behind a thin veil of cologne, vanilla, and cinnamon. It was subtle, like a cup of tea, yet it permeated the air as I stepped away to the center of the lobby. Everything in the hotel lobby looked like an heirloom, like something you'd find in a dusty corner of an antiques shop in Prairie du Chien, Wisconsin, except reupholstered and polished like new. A pair of armchairs on my left, covered

146

in navy and gold chintz and coupled in an inviting way, sat behind a smooth cherry coffee table with magazines spread out in a neat little fan. And across the room a brown leather love seat and two wingback chairs were set in a semicircle around another table. *Come hither,* I thought, *but don't forget your ascot, your pipe, and your monocle.* A splashy pink and white oasis in the center of the room, stuffed with daylilies, stargazers, and tigers, sprouted up between two appropriately ornate chandeliers. Doubting the flowers were real, I leaned in and took a sniff. They were. They smelled like wads of walkin'-around money.

"Jule," Jeremiah called as he mounted the steps toward the centerpiece.

"Hey. Dad's just check—" I stopped and looked him up and down. "Nice outfit."

"I know," he said, and looked down at his clothes. "I had just finished cutting the lawn when Katie picked me up."

His hair had been cut recently, but it was so greasy that for a second I honestly wanted to pretend I didn't know him. He had on a Who jersey and baggy gray sweatpants with a long rip across the thigh that exposed his plaid boxer shorts. The handle of his toothbrush hung out of the right pocket. His penny loafers were caked green with grass clippings and some clung to the tiny hairs around his ankles. He looked like a runaway.

"What's in the bag?" I asked, pointing to the black Hefty bag he had tied around his fist.

"My clothes."

"Those are your good clothes?"

"Yep."

"Nice."

"I know, I know. I couldn't find any luggage at Jimmy and Treasie's."

"Our stuff's on that cart over there," I said, gesturing across the lobby to where the cart was parked between a set of long red damask curtains braided with gold rope. They looked like something Scarlett O'Hara might have ripped down and worn to visit Rhett Butler in jail.

By the time George had finished checking in, Katie and three other women who worked with her in the restaurant's catering division—Wendy, Liz, and Tammy—had arrived. They tossed their luggage on the cart and we all crammed into the tiny elevator with the bellhop. I saw him raise an eyebrow and smile when he noticed Wendy carrying two jugs of chardonnay, one in each hand, her fingers curled under the small glass loop handles. Nothing says swanky like a jug of wine.

We had too many people in the room—that was clear. They kept showing up—Katie's friend Colleen, our brother Stevie, a few wait people from the restaurant. Every time I heard a knock and opened the door, it was like a clown car let out. When my father called down and asked that eight cots be set up for the evening, the guy at the desk finally put his foot down.

"Eight?" I heard a husky voice shout through the receiver. Then I heard it say something about fire codes, and ". . . not a Howard Johnson's," and "perhaps . . . but . . . no other rooms available."

George hung up the phone and looked at me, his mouth stretched into a thin, tight smile and his eyebrows arched as if I were his accomplice. He said, "They're sending up two."

I remember being struck by how deliciously unaware he was. Because we had worked together, because I had seen him standing in his office at the restaurant wearing nothing but his brown support hose and his powder blue boxers, my father had let his unself-conscious side worm its way well past the point of being uncomfortable. I knew he simply didn't care that the hotel staff was, perhaps, at that very moment, pasting WANTED posters bearing our pictures on the wall behind the check-in desks. The notion that none of this really mattered put me, oddly, at ease.

Still, I couldn't help but ask, "Are they gonna kick us out?"

"For heaven's sake, no," he said, and laughed.

That night we went to Nick's Fishmarket for dinner—fifteen of us, I think. Nick's was, and still is, a Chicago landmark, dress-code fancy with white tablecloths; tuxedos; napkins folded like little geisha fans; and lots of different forks, spoons, and glassware. And chilled butter rosettes.

I noticed the butter because it was a big deal in our house. My mother had a thing about it. At any given time, there were two operational butters in our kitchen: a one-pound restaurant block that lived in the corner next to the toaster, and a quarter-pound store-bought stick that lived in the fridge on a Wedgwood dish with a lid. The toaster butter never left the counter. In a constant state of flux and mottled with bread crumbs, it melted and solidified, depending on the temperature inside and out. It was home to three, sometimes four, different knives, caked with grape jelly, cinnamon sugar, braunschweiger, mayonnaise, whatever. The Wedgwood butter, on the other hand, came out only at dinnertime. Something about it made the dinner hour bedlam slightly more bearable for my mother.

They were handmade, the butter rosettes at Nick's, not the mass-produced, metal-pressed kind, and there were no cinnamon toast crumbs. The tablecloth was crisp, clean, and smooth under my palm. I felt grown up, like my first day as pancake girl, and comfortable, if not completely at home, in front of the intricate place setting. The only problem was the smell.

Working the Sunday brunch, surrounded by ten- and twenty-gallon pots of hot boiled shrimp, had scarred something in my olfactory tract the same way the sausage had scarred my thigh. Even today the smell of anything hot, aquatic, and exoskeletal makes my stomach churn and my tongue sweat, like I've just licked the slippery tile floor of a girls' locker room.

But dinner came with its own set of rules, of course, so I had to order some type of crustacean or I'd never hear the end of it. We were not allowed to order anything inappropriate—for example, no cheeseburgers in a Chinese restaurant, no chicken fingers and fries in an Italian place, and no pizza in a seafood restaurant. Nor were we allowed to repeat orders, so if the guy ahead of you ordered something you had your eye on, too bad. You had to pick something else, and quick.

Because he considered it an educational experience, when choosing appetizers my father liked to do quirky things, like ordering everything on the left side of the menu. Dinner was an exercise in endurance, pacing, and prudence— like running a marathon, except your pants grew tight enough to inhibit circulation. Barrels of beer and wine were followed by wagon trains of appetizers, entrées, and desserts. The thrill of another harrowing dining experience, and the agony of hideous flatulence, inevitably came on the heels of the check. George flipped open the black leather folder and said, "Who wants to guess?" We all did. Whoever came closest without going over had to pay. Guessing the bill was part of the deal. He passed around torn slips of paper and we all wrote down our answers. I can't remember who won, but I do remember the bill being in the neighborhood of twelve hundred dollars. But George paid. He always did.

We decided to take a cab back to the hotel. As soon as the key turned in the lock, bodies lurched toward beds, chairs, love seats, and cots, everyone looking to secure a spot to sleep off dinner. I found my father tucked in the corner of his room, sitting on a love seat, reading. I lay down on his bed and watched him read. There was something peaceful about the way he connected with a book. He kept this weird little smile on his face, like a toddler was whispering something in his ear.

He leaned over and picked up an empty can of Planters peanuts that was sitting on top of a *Where Chicago* magazine. "What's this?"

"Uh, a can of peanuts."

He turned it upside down and let the peanut dust fall onto the coffee table and the carpeting. "It's empty."

"Looks like it."

"Where'd these come from?" Twitch.

"The minibar, I guess."

Then, in a long, guttural, slow-motion moan, he said, "Who said you kids could open the minibar?" For a second I thought he was having a stroke, or maybe *I* was having a stroke.

"Dad?"

His ears, siphoning the wine from the veins in his cheeks, went bloodred.

"What's the matter, Dad?"

"Do you have any idea how expensive these are?"

Because of the way his jaw was clenched, I knew this wasn't really a question. I inched my way backward across the bedspread, just in case I needed to scramble for the door.

"Do you?"

"Um . . ."

"Seven dollars!" Major spine-twisting twitch. "They're SEVEN DOLLARS A CAN!"

"Dad, I—"

"Who opened these?"

"I don't know, Dad. Not me," I said, which really was the truth, but I knew I had created a damaging ripple effect. "Not me" only planted the seeds of frustration in my father, which grew exponentially with each and every subsequent "not me." The first guy to say it was typically in the clear, but it landed everyone else in deep shit. Sometimes, though, you just have to save yourself.

As he marched, empty peanut can wrapped in

his paw, into the other room to interrogate the others, I did a little math.

The hotel room.

"WHO ATE THESE?"

Plus the dinner.

"Who?"

Plus the drinks.

"These aren't *free,* you know."

Plus the walkin'-around money.

"That minibar is off-limits. Understand. *Do you understand?"*

I heard a quiet round of yesses and knew everyone was trying not to laugh. It sounds terrible, I know, but his breaking-point tantrums invariably had a morsel that made keeping a straight face next to impossible. George didn't prepare for hysteria. When his veins started popping, it didn't matter if his hair was standing on end, if his face was half covered with shaving cream, or if he was in his underwear. He just let it rip, and what you saw was what you got. That night, because of the enormous dinner, he had taken his belt off and unbuttoned his pants.

The next morning he walked down Michigan Avenue to a Walgreens, bought a can of Walgreens-brand peanuts, brought them back, and placed them in the minibar just so. It never occurred to him that the person who restocked the thing might notice the slight difference in brands and charge him anyway. Again, how do you keep a straight face? You tell me. Of course, no one ever confessed to the peanut mistake. Unbuttoned pants or not, eating a *seven-dollar* can of peanuts was a serious offense. Simply put, they were not ours to eat. We had no business opening that minibar. Whoever ate those peanuts has managed to keep their mouth shut to this day. Had it been me, I'm not sure I would have confessed. I'm not sure I would even now.

Pandl's brunch. From left to right: George, Jeremiah, Amy, Johnny, Chrissy, Peggy, Stevie, Katie, Jimmy, and Julie.

George and Terry leaving their wedding.

The family. In back, left to right: Jimmy, Johnny, Jeremiah, Katie, Julie; in front, left to right: Stevie, Amy, Peggy, Chrissy.

Terry and
George.

George's eightieth birthday at Jack Pandl's. From left to right: Peggy, Chrissy, Johnny, Amy, George, Julie, Katie, Stevie, Jeremiah, and Jimmy.

PART II

What are we to make of Christ?
There is no question of what we can make of Him,
it is entirely a question of what
He intends to make of us.
You must accept or reject the story.

—C. S. Lewis

10

From There to Here

As I reached for a set of sheets on the top shelf of my linen closet, the hair on my arm brushed against the soft plastic end of a warped flyswatter. It hung on a crooked nail. I supposed I had put it there, though I had no recollection of doing so. I pulled it from its hook, rolled the bent wire handle around my fingers, and heard a voice in my memory saying, *Can we leave that for the new people?*

It was George. The two of us were standing on a musty-smelling bed of flattened rhubarb behind the garage in Oostburg, staring at an upside-down rusty bathtub. A jigsaw puzzle of yellow paint had chipped away from the tub's underbelly, and black moss sprouted around the claw feet on one end. My mother loved that tub. The thing had made the move from Milwaukee to Cedar Grove and then to Oostburg. It was a little piece of Prospect Avenue, a classic leftover from a remodeling job of the boys' bathroom. Each time the movers hauled it from the back of their van, before telling them to put it behind the garage, she talked of restoring it to its original beauty and putting it to use. I was pretty sure the

163

new people wouldn't need it, but certain also that lifting it would reveal something with beady eyes and razor-sharp teeth. I said, "Yeah, I'm thinking we can."

That little exchange between my father and me happened a hundred times that day. He pointed to or picked up a thing, raised his eyebrows for approval, and I nodded. It began with the flyswatter, of course—because it was just wrong to pack that with bedsheets and bath towels—and it grew to include the dead geraniums in the plant room, broken rakes, rusty handsaws, a box of tangled fishing tackle, and a dusty stack of phone books in the workshop next to the garage.

It was a Saturday in October 1999, and my parents were moving from Oostburg back to Milwaukee. In the weeks, months, even years leading up to the move, I had watched my parents slide past their prime and into old age. I had come and gone, finished high school, attended college, worked at the restaurant and elsewhere, but the fact that they were growing older always compelled me to stay nearby. I guess I figured at some point they might need me, and a little part of me knew they wouldn't be around forever.

My father had retired and unretired at least fifteen times. He sold the restaurant to my brother Jimmy, in 1987, my junior year in high school, and retired. Six months later, he bought a restaurant in Chilton, Wisconsin, and within two years the place had gobbled up his and my mother's life savings. It wasn't pretty, watching my father fail. It left him shell-shocked, broken. For months he walked around befuddled, fretting about how to get the place sold while my mother buried statues of St. Joseph and said novenas. Years later, he told me that the day he used the last of my college education fund to pay his bills was the day he decided to close the restaurant's doors.

It's interesting how much light a little darkness can shed. Even back then, as a senior in high school and a freshman in college, I saw it. The notion of my parents' impending financial doom made me nervous, so I watched. Plus, it was just the three of us, so what else was I going to do? We cursed that restaurant in Chilton daily. My mother cursed the drive, the town, and everyone in it, but the business and its demise had a lasting purpose in my father's life. He stumbled and fell while doing what he had done his entire life, doing what he did best, and it changed him. I watched, and I saw him stand up and choose humility over bitterness in the face of failure.

Lest you think I was wise beyond my years, I have to confess this insight was helped along by the fact that the same year my father bought the restaurant in Chilton, I flunked chemistry. I was cocky and I thought I knew things. Accustomed to classes that required a certain amount of bullshitting, I just didn't believe my teacher when he said we had to learn the periodic table in order for anything else to make sense. Turned out, he wasn't bullshitting. I know it's not the same—fiscal disaster in your midsixties and flunking eleventh-grade chemistry—but tell that to any high school junior and see what he or she says, especially these days. If you're a parent, you might want to have your checkbook ready for the therapist. At any rate, my father made me take chemistry again my senior year, so I was familiar with the concept of humility riding on the heels of failure. I got a C the second time around, and with that, I crossed scientist and engineer off my list of possible careers.

After the debacle in Chilton my father retired again, but it didn't take, so he got a volunteer job delivering phone books for the town of Wilson, just east of Oostburg. He thought it would be a nice part-time gig, something to do when he wasn't reading and in those times when Terry needed him out of her hair. Two days into the job, on a ruthlessly cold and snowy January evening, I found him in the garage. His butt poked out of the open driver's side door as he leaned in and searched around the floor under the steering wheel.

"Dad?"

"Yeah." His voice was muffled underneath the hood of his big winter coat.

"What are you doing?" I asked.

"I lost my goddamned glove."

"Huh?"

He pulled himself out. His hair twisted in a brittle, wiry pile, a combination of frozen sweat and whatever men's hair gel was on sale at Walgreens. "Well," he said, gesturing with his gloved hand to the phone books scattered across the backseat, "I was delivering the phone books, and I hit a patch of ice on the road and slid the car into a row of goddamned mailboxes. Look at this." He slammed the door, walked around the car, and pointed to where the mailboxes had left a messy white gash in the paint above the wheel well. The side mirror dangled from two thin wires. He lifted it and let it drop.

"Are you okay?"

"Yeah, yeah, I'm fine."

"What about the mailboxes?"

"I tried to fix them. I stood out there for half an hour, but it's colder than hell, and I lost my glove. I thought I was gonna freeze to death."

"So, did you leave the mailboxes in a pile or what?"

"I stood them up in the snowbank. They're fine," he said, opening the back door and grabbing a stack of phone books. "Here, help me with these."

"What are you going do with them?"

"Stack 'em up in the workshop."

I already knew the answer, but I asked anyway. "Are you ever going to deliver them?"

"You've got to be kidding me. Absolutely not. Absolutely *not*." He slapped the single soft brown leather glove on the roof of the car. "This ridiculous job has already cost me a pair of expensive gloves, wrecked my car, and damn near killed me. Who needs new phone books anyway? They can use their old ones."

That was it. The stack of phone books collected dust, spiderwebs, and mouse droppings in the corner of the workshop, and they stayed behind when my parents moved from Oostburg back to Milwaukee. Perhaps they're still there.

The new people didn't need the phone books, of course, or any of the other crap, but neither did Terry and George. They were downsizing to a one-level ranch-style house in Bayside, one that had wide hallways with plenty of room for my mother's wheelchair, one that was closer to the restaurant, one that was closer to us kids. The new house came on the heels of the amputation of my mother's left foot. Diabetes had brought a swift and decisive end to the long debate regarding the move back to Milwaukee. The very thing that allowed her to move from one place to another had been cut off, and that—*that*—finally caused them to make the move. The irony, it kills me.

• • •

BY THE TIME moving day rolled around we were all exhausted. My father and I wheeled Terry down the flagstone walk and helped her pivot into the passenger's seat of my car. I tossed the wheelchair and her temporary prosthetic in the backseat, buckled myself in next to her, and said, "You ready?"

Her voice quivered when she said, "I guess so."

I looked over and saw tears welling up in her eyes. Having so little left to offer, and afraid something as sardonic as "snap out of it" might come out of my mouth, I put the car in reverse and backed onto the gravel drive. We were in a hurry. That's what I told myself. I had to drive her into Milwaukee and drop her off at the new house, where Katie and Peggy were waiting, and then drive back out to Oostburg and help George and the movers pack up the old house. That was all true, but there was something else in the urgency I felt. I think it was fear, ragged and raw. Fear that I had squelched since the day she first mentioned the sore, and I saw the look in her eyes.

She held her hand out as we weaved our way through the trees. I gave it a quick squeeze and pulled mine away to make the turn onto Wilson Lima. The road was empty, as always. Dry cornstalks, waiting to be harvested, leaned over in the north wind.

"Are you sad?" I asked.

"A little bit, yes."

"I'm surprised."

"Me too." She pressed her fist into her left thigh, rubbing it back and forth.

"Are you scared?"

"I am a little."

I swallowed the lump in my throat. I was haunted by my own ignorance. She had mentioned the sore and then showed it to me a few days later. I drove her to the doctor; he put her on antibiotics and sent her home. I didn't know a tiny sore, the size of a pencil eraser, could, despite hefty antibiotics, become something so hideous, so gruesome. The fight that ensued defied description.

I steadied the steering wheel. Glancing over my right shoulder to switch lanes, I caught a glimpse of the fake foot, wearing her tennis shoe.

The day we knew the fight was over, I was the one who made the call. It sticks with you, making that kind of judgment call. I wanted to curl up in the corner and suck my thumb; instead, I stood next to my father and watched the visiting nurse unravel puffy loops of white gauze. I remember she had kinky blond hair and wore gold-rimmed glasses. A stethoscope hung around her neck, and a blood pressure cuff spilled from the pocket of a corduroy blazer. She had a pink binder with my mother's name written in the top right corner, and a pen advertising something called Detrol LA. All the right instruments required for taking and recording one's state of being. None of it mattered, though. Terry had been spiking fevers—102, 103, 104 degrees—throughout the previous couple of days, which we thought meant a new infection was brewing somewhere. As soon as the nurse peeled the last bits of dressing off my mother's foot, we knew.

It didn't bleed. That was the problem. Infection, followed by a barbaric process called debridement, had literally swallowed pieces of my mother's foot in random yet measured increments.

"It looks good, huh?" the nurse said.

"Good?" I gasped. What looked good to her, to this very day, makes me want to cover even my mind's eye.

"Yeah, look here." She pointed with her pen to a taut yellow tendon.

George twitched, pulled his lips between his teeth, and clasped his hands behind his head. My mother looked down at her foot, looked up at him, and then at me. Her face was round, waxy, and pale. Her lips, usually never without a perfect whisper of pink, were thin and colorless. She pleaded, not out loud, but with her eyes.

"It's going to be okay, Mom." I smiled and nodded.

She had not been herself—she had not been *my* mother—for months. Pain medication, infection, and worry mugged her little by little every day, stealing her confidence, her wit, her soul. I had not seen her smile in a week. She was fidgety and obsessed about where things were and what time it was. She carried a travel alarm clock around in her pocket and checked it every ten minutes. Her rosary had to be placed just so on her nightstand, every night, despite the fact that she couldn't concentrate long enough to get through the first sentence of a Hail Mary.

I looked down the length of her skinny calf and saw angry red streaks creeping up toward her knee. There was no noise except my heart beating in my eardrums.

"Dad," I said, turning to him, "we're calling the doctor."

He stared at me. His brow furrowed.

I took his elbow and pulled him into the kitchen. "If we don't do something about that foot, Dad, she's going to die. This is it. We can't fight it anymore. Today's the day."

He just stared at me.

"Dad."

"Okay. Call."

So I grabbed the phone off the kitchen wall, found the doctor's number scribbled on a piece of loose-leaf paper on the counter, and called. Then I went downstairs, used the phone outside the laundry room to call Katie, and told her to meet us at the doctor's office.

A week later, when we stood in a semicircle around her hospital bed and Terry made a wisecrack about getting a half-price pedicure, my insides finally stopped shaking.

WHEN WE PULLED into the driveway at the new house, Katie and Peggy were outside on the patio, sitting in broken plastic chairs the previous owner had left "for the new people." The house was empty except for a few boxes of small stuff and some breakables that we had already moved. It smelled like dog. I wondered how long it would take before I walked in and smelled them—citrus, vanilla, and Ammens powder. I wheeled Terry into the family room and parked her next to the Wedgwood lamp. "I'm going to go back out and help Dad with the movers. We should be here late this afternoon."

"Where's my leg?"

"It's right here, Mom." Katie held it up and set it in the bay window that faced the patio. "Let's put the lampshade on it."

Terry burst out laughing and said, "Oh, you kids are such brats."

It was unlucky timing, and circumstance, really, me being the one who had to make that call. Always and forever the baby, though, I took mental and verbal measurements against what my siblings might have done. Everyone agreed it was the right thing to do. Clearly there was no question. We got her back, for a while anyway, not the whole of her, but the best parts—the spirit, the smile, and the wit. Truth be told, though, none of us was completely whole again; at least I wasn't. The loss of that foot somehow left me unbalanced. Never again did I lean on my mother for help with anything. I simply decided she couldn't handle the weight.

11

Shalimar

My mother peed in a pot last night. Well, it's not a pot, exactly; it's a stainless steel bowl with a handle and units of measurement on the side. She straddled the pot/bowl that my sister Katie held so carefully, so accurately.

We brought her home from the hospital, Katie, George, and I. He banged around the kitchen while we watched *Wheel of Fortune*. I hate *Wheel of Fortune* now. It was so much better when the contestants had to spend their winnings on leather furniture, fake floral arrangements, and ceramic dogs. "I'll take the his-and-hers matching jogging suits for one thousand, Pat." Terry loves it, though, so what are you going to do? My parents are in their seventies now, older, so the TV is loud enough to wake the dead.

We had my mother's foot propped up on a wooden chair with wheels from the kitchen table. We cushioned it with a throw pillow, embroidered with blue hearts and daisies, a gift from Mary, my artsy-craftsy sister-in-law. It was wrapped in gauze, that foot, like a giant Q-tip. As soon as George closed the bathroom door, she had to go.

Naturally, the knob on the bathroom door was broken.

I had one foot on the ground outside the window and one foot on the first rung of the ladder, a hammer in one hand and a wrench in the other. My father quietly fiddled with the knob while Terry cried and peed.

I hope against hope, keep my fingers crossed, I cross my heart and hope to die.

But I'm already in a place where I know better.

In the morning I can hear them talking above me, she and my father. Their bedroom is just above mine.

Mumbling.

I wonder if they're lying in bed, holding hands, hoping. Or maybe they don't need hope; maybe they just know that everything will be all right. After all, everything always has been.

My room is cold and dark except for my flannel sheets pulled over my nose and a stream of morning sunlight pouring in from the window in the corner. I don't sleep at home that often anymore, only when they need me.

I can't need them anymore.

It's safe down here in the basement, my bunker, my cocoon. The world stays still; it's quiet except for the mumbling. It's their sound, waking up together yet again. How many days have they done this? Forty-six years' worth of days and then some, I think. They chat. I don't know what about. It's warm in their bed too; I've been there—flannel sheets, down comforter, and the warmth of my father holding my mother's hand. Maybe they chat about me, maybe they chat about the other kids, maybe they chat about the restaurant or the Catholic church. I don't know, but I know they chat and hold hands.

IT'S A DIABETIC ulcer on the ball of that foot, the left one, below the big toe, where the energy from the kidneys flows. A few weeks ago, as we waited for my father to bring the car around, she said, "I have a thing on my foot."

"What kind of thing?"

"I don't know, a little sore."

That's when I lost her. My mother disappeared right in front of me, standing on the curb outside the Broadway Theater, waiting for my father to bring the car around. I saw the worry in her eyes, gray and green, churning like the lake toward shore on a windy fall day. That worry she had always reserved for us; those eyes were on her now. It was icy cold, February 1999. The wind took our breath away.

I worried too, then, and made my mother disappear.

MY MOTHER TOLD me she'd watch over me from up above. Then I brushed her hair.

My mother took me to look at colleges. We smoked cigs, drank Diet Pepsi, and drove across Iowa on I-80.

My mother has pneumonia again.

My mother was lonely.

MY MOTHER HAD her foot amputated yesterday. I asked what they did with amputated feet. No one answered.

My mother died this morning.

My mother made peace in our family. She farted, little putt-putts during tense family meetings about the restaurant, and we laughed.

My mother had a lung biopsy today, and died on the table, but only for a minute.

MY MOTHER HAD a heart attack today.

My mother married my father in 1952. He proposed in front of the Marian Shrine on Sixty-eighth Street in Milwaukee. He gave her a rosary and she said yes.

My mother let me skip school today. She took me shopping and out to lunch.

My mother was lonely.

SHE PRAYED TO St. Thérèse, the Little Flower. The roses always came, yet George doubted.

She mailed a care package to Peggy at college. She filled it with Mrs. Becherer's underwear. Found forgotten in a drawer in the Cedar Grove house. No cookies, no candy, just big beige granny panties.

She smoked. She loved smoking and she loved smokers.

My mother smelled pretty, like Shalimar.

She wore lipstick every single day, and not on her teeth. She blotted it on a single sheet of tissue and dropped it in the toilet, like a floating kiss.

MY MOTHER HAS pneumonia again.

My mother danced. She danced the grandma dance, twirling her small hands while sitting in a chair.

She made wildly funny faces.

She left a half banana on the kitchen counter every day.

My mother quit smoking for Lent and took up knitting.

She did the crossword every morning. She pulled words out of the sky.

My mother was lonely.

• • •

SHE PRAYED TO St. Thérèse. *Little Flower, show your power. Let fall from heaven a shower of roses.* George doubted.

My mother let me skip school today and took me shopping and out to lunch.

My mother drank her coffee black. She gave up sugar for Lent one year and creamer the next year.

She had shoes, tons of shoes.

She was lonely.

SHE PRAYED. HE doubted.

She loved Buick station wagons. She said they were safe.

My mother paced and prayed the Memorare. *Remember, O most gracious Virgin Mary . . .*

She had small hands, soft, hands made to be held.

She asked a lot of questions during movies. Holy shit, did she ask questions.

She was lonely.

MY MOTHER CRIED forty-three-year-old tears when she found out she was pregnant with me. She was in labor for four days.

My mother peed in a pot last night.

She left a half banana on the counter.

My mother told me she'd watch over me from up above. Then I brushed her hair.

MY MOTHER DIED this morning. It's Johnny's fiftieth birthday, November 14, 2002. She had a look in her eyes I didn't recognize, vacant and mechanical. She was already gone. We held her hands and prayed, Katie, George, and I. I mumbled the Memorare, asking the Blessed Mother to take her hand. She disappeared in the night. Her soul floated, and she kissed us while we slept.

SHE SMELLED PRETTY, like Shalimar.

12

The Promise

We made a deathbed promise, Katie and Peggy and I. Our mother wasn't actually dying at the time, but you know that promise when you make it, deathbed or not.

We were at St. Mary's Hospital in Ozaukee. The room smelled of soap, sweet and antiseptic.

She said, "Keep an eye on Daddy," and the air got sucked out of the room. I tried to sneak a little breath before it happened, but it was like someone sucker punched me right in the gut and stuck a wool sock in my throat.

"Okay," we said, immediately, emphatically. I mean, really, what were we going to say?

You'll know it when you hear it—it changes everything—and you won't say no either.

"KEEP AN EYE on Daddy."

An ambiguous request, open to interpretation, followed by a promise. A request that left us a little wiggle room.

Ours was a loose working definition. "Keep an eye on Daddy," we thought, was code for "Make sure he doesn't leave the house looking like a hobo." She knew better, though; she knew more.

We stretch the boundaries, or maybe they stretch on their own.

The line between her words and our actions is wobbly, not what it used to be.

We do shoddy work, but he listens.

He leaves the house looking like a hobo, daily. Dressed in kelly green shorts, a white T-shirt, red suspenders, black socks pulled up to his knees, and tan shoes. He runs to the hardware store, to Bayside Garden Center, Schwartz Bookstore, and Walgreens.

He's seventy-seven now. He married my mother fifty years ago, nearly fifty-one. He proposed with a rosary and she said yes.

HE DRINKS TWO martinis, not three.
He grieves.

He wears white vinyl exam gloves wherever he goes, an effort to kick his habit of picking his hangnails. He walks into the bank like he always has, through the mahogany entryway and past the velvety nubuck leather furniture, up to the dark marble counter of the teller windows, looking not only like a hobo but also kind of creepy, like he has a chopped-up body stashed in the trunk.

He's back, working at the restaurant, has been for quite a while.

He chef pants are rolled up around his shins.

"Keep an eye on Daddy."

HE DRINKS TWO martinis, not three.

He actually does know how to dress, feigning ignorance all these years just to push Terry's buttons. Just like a husband.

He's faithful to the core, although he doesn't admit it. He champions all religions.

He made each of us a collage; a picture of us with Terry in the middle, high school graduation, vacationing in Door County, sitting on her lap. He got the babies all mixed up. Mine has a picture of Katie; hers has a picture of me. Jimmy's has a picture of Stevie and Stevie's has Jeremiah. These pictures made when we were babies had a sameness. We are harder to define without her.

He grieves.

• • •

HE TAKES LONG walks. He climbs the lookout tower at the Audubon Center.

He has Jean Feraca's birthday on his calendar. Who the hell *is* that? And *why* does he need to remember her birthday?

He eats bowls of bleu cheese with a cocktail fork.

He crushes boxes at the restaurant.

He showed up the other day with half of his front tooth missing.

"Keep an eye on Daddy."

HE PICKS HIS hangnails until they bleed. He's afraid he can't be a good guest without her.

We, Katie and Peggy and I, told him never to show up empty-handed.

Loneliness bears gifts.

He brings pretty soaps from Caswell-Massey to parties as a gift for the hostess, and the host.

He stopped murdering squirrels.

HE USES MASKING tape and a Sharpie to mark foil-wrapped items in the freezer—ham, chicken livers, tenderloin tips—with the day and the year.

He reads.

He uses Pink Pearl body shampoo on everything: his dishes, his floors, his body, his hair.

183

He wraps books from his library in newspaper and gives them to us for Christmas.

He wraps junk from his garage in newspaper and gives it to us for Christmas. We all got an orange plastic pasta fork.

He stopped going to Mass.

"Keep an eye on Daddy."

HE CRUSHES BOXES at the restaurant.

He cuts out tiny pictures of roses and tapes them to the front of envelopes containing birthday cards.

He eats spearmint leaves and drinks sherry in bed.

He drinks two martinis, not three.

He grieves.

HE WASHES THE car for the first time ever, gets a haircut, and goes out on a "date."

He puts the milk jug right on the kitchen table.

He takes us to Spring Green, to the American Players Theatre, the House on the Rock, and the National Mustard Museum, all of us—the boys, the girls, and the grandchildren. He gives us all embroidered old-lady change purses with walkin'-around money inside.

He reads.

HE BUYS CASWELL-MASSEY soap by the gross.

Loneliness bears gifts.

He drives the car, with its TERRY P license plates and PRAY THE ROSARY bumper sticker.

He stops going to Mass.

"Keep an eye on Daddy."

He's a boxer-brief man now, Calvin Klein; they have to be Calvin Klein.

He changes his sheets with the seasons.

HE DRINKS TWO martinis, not three.

He spends the entire summer walking around the house wearing only his Calvin Kleins.

He picks his hangnails until they bleed.

He grieves.

He stops going to Mass. He's faithful to the core.

He's creating change, exacting meaning.

The promise came with a big hole; still, there's no room for sameness anymore.

13

Hocus-Pocus

Our parents are planted everywhere in us—their smiles, their gait, their stomachs, their habits. The older we get, the stronger the roots. Our resistance is worn down with wisdom, and in time we begin to do things, like replace the empty toilet paper roll with a new one. We buy pants with elastic waistbands; we turn the lights off and the heat down; we change the sheets and set out fresh towels for our guests. In time we become what we said we never would—we become them—and we smile in spite of ourselves.

My mother planted the seeds of faith in our family and did the lion's share of the watering. Hers was a simple two-step process, both gentle and fierce, strangely naive and knowledgeable. She began by bringing the church to us. The Holy Family and the Communion of Saints were ever present in our house, in our cars, and on our person. Tiny icons traveled with and among us, watching us eat, sleep, fight, pray, and live. Gladly handing over her Rolodex of short prayers, rosaries, and novenas, she taught us who to call, and how, when intercession was beyond our control. The Crucified Christ hung around our necks and over our beds, St. Christopher and the Sacred Heart of Jesus dangled together from safety pins pressed into vinyl car visors, the Infant of Prague looked faithfully out the window on the eve of every outdoor party, bringing good weather; the concrete St. Anne stood sentry, facing east, beckoning sailors safely to shore; and St. Joseph was buried upside down in the backyard of every home being prepared for sale.

They were all respected and welcome additions

to our family, with one exception. I was eight or nine, I guess, when Jimmy came home from a trip out west, bearing a life-size portrait of Jesus with the Crown of Thorns, inked in thick, midnight blue velvet. Even I could see that using velvet as a canvas to depict the Lord was a practice that needed restriction under canon law. It was novelty-shop tacky in a way that at once insulted both God and novelty shops. A gift from her prodigal son, my mother hung it nonetheless, in the front foyer, just inside the door we never used, and Jesus laughed.

She wouldn't admit it, but she had two favorites: the Blessed Mother and St. Thérèse of Lisieux. She had an extraordinary bond with these two women; theirs was a closeness found only in faith. Identifying with Mary in motherhood and with St. Thérèse in name, she referred to them as her "buds." Mary accompanied my mother as she paced around the dining room table, hundreds of thousands of times, wearing her cotton nightgown and mumbling the Memorare, waiting for someone to give birth to a baby, get through surgery, or more often than not, complete a long drive home from college in a snowstorm.

And St. Thérèse, the Little Flower, brought roses without fail on the heels of every novena. She comforted my mother when earthly comforts were exhausted, when we were exhausted. Her hand-painted six-inch replica, sealed in a Ziploc freezer bag along with my mother's rosary and hairbrush, made dozens of trips into and out of the hospital. We all witnessed the call, "Little Flower, show your power," that brought my mother over the hurdle of amputation. St. Thérèse stood by when it was time for the rest of us to go home, watching my mother from her place on the adjustable bedside tray table. She held my mother's trust, her heart, and her hand. These friendships, born of faith, set us on the path of believing without seeing.

Step two in Terry's catechism brought us to church. Regular attendance at Sunday Mass was nonnegotiable in the same way that breathing is nonnegotiable. My mother knew the secret that formed the unshakable bond of faith: practice. It was that simple. We went to Mass and we received the sacraments. We did not question, argue, or even discern. There was nothing touchy-feely, nothing "up to us" about it. We just went. If we did not go, and were not behind bars or in a full body cast, bleeding out our eyes, we swung by St. Robert's and picked up a weekly bulletin. If we did not get a chance to pick up a bulletin, we lied—at least I did, and I'm fairly certain the rest of my siblings did too. I was thirty before I could look my mother in the eye and confess that I missed the occasional Sunday Mass. And even as I explained that her work was done—that I was a practicing, albeit somewhat erratically, Catholic—I felt the sting of offending her and Jesus.

George was wired differently when it came to religion. He was on board in the Mass department, of course. He sat in the driveway and honked the horn on Sunday mornings, and even corralled us into the front pew at St. Robert's, all the while reading books like *The Secret Archives of the Vatican*, *The Church That Forgot Christ*, *The Daily Dilemma of the Christian*, *In Defense of Secular Humanism*, and *How the Pope Became Infallible*. He searched for faith, waiting for it to come together in a neat little sentence and jump off the page, hoping to solve the mystery by contradicting its essence. He believed in God and prayed often. He also believed in, and even cherished, Holy Communion. He accepted the presence of Jesus Christ in the simple fellowship of breaking bread. It spoke to him on a familial level. The wheels came off, though, when it came to the hierarchy of the church. He did not, he could not, believe in an institution run solely by men, with no system of checks and balances. The pope went against George's grain. He called the church the only absolute monarchy, and he constantly questioned its authority and wealth. Yet he practiced.

Conflicted, and offended to the core by the

189

political and religious apathy that spawned the Holocaust, he owned—more than most Catholics, I think—our Jewish roots, and taught us to do the same. Judaism has no pope; it also has female rabbis. Therefore, Judaism appealed to his skeptical nature and his feminine side. He embraced the traditions, verbal and edible, with gusto—attempting Hebrew, gobbling up gefilte fish, and preparing beef brisket on Christmas Day when my mother insisted on ham. How they ever managed to present a united front and raise an ever-expanding army of practicing Catholics is a mystery the Holy See might want to look into.

SIX MONTHS BEFORE my mother died, Memorial Day weekend of 2002, Chrissy's brother-in-law, Dan Griffith, was ordained into the priesthood in St. Paul, Minnesota. Holy Orders happened often enough, but it was rare to actually know someone joining the team. When the invitation came, my mother was pensively excited. Like most Catholic mothers, she had always wanted one of her sons to become a priest, but none of them had the calling. So she quickly claimed Dan as one of her own. She pulled down the family portrait—the one of the nine of us huddled together on a frigid fall day at Hubbard Park—from its prominent place in the center of the refrigerator, cast it aside with a flick

190

of her wrist, and slipped Dan's invitation into its place. She smoothed it down with her puffy, prednisone-swollen hand and told George, "We're going, come hell or high water." He rolled his eyes.

My parents never traveled light, especially when we were kids. Because there were eleven of us, we didn't fly many places, so they had the luxury of packing the car as if they had been commissioned to map a newly discovered, uninhabited continent. My father packed books, sometimes as many as ten or twenty, in empty wine boxes from the restaurant. He also packed booze, wine, and sherry—always sherry—in the same boxes. Without the sherry, their nighttime sleep routine was disrupted in a way that tended to ruin the following day. Terry packed every-thing else: clothes, shoes, hats, scarves, mittens, jackets, snow pants, boots, skis, bathing suits, beach towels, and sunscreen, depending on the destination and the time of year.

The trip to St. Paul was different only insofar as we were old enough to take separate cars, caravanning west and then north on I-94, plus my mother had been flirting with the angel of death for some months. He had taken her for a spin around the dance floor on several occasions but had retreated each time, leaving behind a new medical apparatus for her to contend with: an oxygen tank, a wheelchair, a commode, a titanium leg, or what have you. We knew, and perhaps she did too, it was only a matter of time before he left the deathbed, so the pilgrimage to the Catholic Super Bowl became charged, ironically, with life.

Peggy and I followed behind as their Blessed Virgin blue Buick dragged along the asphalt, weighted down with the oxygen tank, the wheelchair, the commode, the titanium leg, the books, and the sherry. The car was a pharmacy on wheels, equipped for anything from diarrhea to diabetic shock, and all aches, pains, and respiratory distresses in between. I remember watching the PRAY THE ROSARY bumper sticker bounce in time with the bumps in the road, laughing at what a shamelessly obvious metaphor my mother had created for my father to drive.

We arrived at the Holiday Inn in downtown St. Paul at about six o'clock on Friday. It was a sunny afternoon, with a temperature that anywhere else in the world would be considered a little chilly for the end of May, but it was warmly welcome by Twin Cities standards. Winter had finally stopped haunting spring, and the crooked branches of the cottonwoods were shrouded in bright yellowy green. My father pulled the car up to the curb in front of the revolving glass door, and we pulled up behind them. I stepped out of the car into a sea of cousins. The sidewalk hummed with the excited chatter of togetherness. Our families combined into a strangely twisted vine of relatives and friends. When Chrissy married Bill, Dan's brother, who was also the first cousin of our sister-in-law Treasie, things got complicated in a way that isn't worth unwinding here. Suffice it to say that, over the years generations of Griffiths and Pandls have shared everything from high school hallways and college dorm rooms to cousins, aunts, uncles, and grandparents.

Wrapped up in hug after hug, I made my way over to my parents' car and commenced the unloading. George pulled the wheelchair out of the backseat and unfolded it on the curb while Terry handed me her portable oxygen tank and Peggy hauled suitcases and wine boxes from the trunk. My mother pivoted herself over to the wheelchair and plopped down with a frustrated wince. "Ouch, ouch, ouch! This damn back." I winced too. Presumably a side effect from a hip replacement the previous February, her severe and chronic back pain was a recent development.

"Here, Mom, lemme get your feet in the things," I said, squatting down and turning the footrests flat. She had on a spring jacket, pastel plaid, and a pair of slacks that were roomy around the ankles. "Are you okay?"

"Yes, yes. Hand me my purse, will you, please?"

"Hang on a sec, Mom, let me just . . . get these right."

She wiggled, anxious to join the flurry of hellos. I straightened her pants legs, leaned into the car, and grabbed her purse off the floor of the front seat. By the time I turned around, purse in hand, she had circled her wheelchair into a flock of cousins, aunts, and uncles. I stood watching her. Her profile showed a soft, cheeky smile as she planted a hand and a kiss on the face of an old friend. My mother was a great guest at a party, easy, one of those people whose worries melted away in a crowd. On her sickest day, I'd take a conversation with her, in a corner over a glass of chardonnay, before most people. Chaos softened her. She forgot herself, sidled up with a drink and a cigarette, patted you on the knee, and became a gentle confidante. People loosened their caps around her, and she around them.

"Here, Mom." I reached through the crowd and over her shoulder to put her purse on her lap. "I'm gonna help Dad."

In our haste to get the Buick-cum-Medivan unpacked, Peggy, George, and I left an unmistakable signal on the curb outside the Holiday Inn. It was my brother Jimmy who discovered it. It could have been left anywhere in the world, really—on the banks of the Thames, next to the Blarney Stone, under the Eiffel Tower—and my parents' presence would have been felt. There, on the edge of a sidewalk in St. Paul, two days before Dan Griffith took his vow, sat a lonely commode with the top flipped open and two bottles of sherry waiting patiently in the bucket, an icon of George and Terry's fifty-year marriage, of togetherness in sickness and in health.

THE SOFTNESS THAT came with the chaos had a tendency to disappear once only one or two of us were with Terry. Pain became worry, and worry folded itself in my mother's brow and behind her eyes. As we drove over to Chrissy and Bill's for the preparty, Terry shifted her tiny bottom around the impossible velour car seat, unable to find a pain-free position.

"Agh! My back hurts, my leg hurts, everything hurts. *Everything,*" she said, pressing both legs into the floor and clutching the door handle.

My father sat in the backseat, reading something about spirituality for the skeptic.

"Mom, just stop moving around. We'll be there in five minutes."

"There it is. Turn left at the lights," she directed. She laid her hand calmly against the window. "Look, it's so beautiful."

"Yeah, it's pretty, Mom," I agreed, turning left onto John Ireland Drive and eyeballing the Cathedral of St. Paul under the visor. It was— pretty, I mean. I'd seen it dozens of times before, of course, but still, its boldly out-of-place magnificence gave me goose bumps. The granite facade of the entryway had a soft pinkish hue in the lights, and the steeple atop the copper dome had grown dark under the shadows of the early evening sky.

"George, look, isn't it beautiful?"

He raised his head, looked over, and said with a long sigh, "I wonder what it would cost to build that thing today—a hundred million, two hundred," and went back to his reading. The cathedral disappeared as we headed up Summit Avenue.

She squirmed again. "Ugh."

"Mom, stop, seriously."

She reached in her purse, pulled out a transparent orange prescription bottle, opened it, and let out an anxious gasp. "Oh my God, no! George, I've only got two pain pills left." She turned to me and shook the bottle to illustrate the hideous sound made by two measly pills bouncing around hollow plastic.

"Did you fill the prescription, George? Did you pack the refill?"

I checked the rearview mirror and saw my father reach his knobby hand up and peel it across his forehead. Shit.

"Son of a *biscuit*." Twitch.

"Oh, George, you didn't."

"No, I'm sorry. I forgot."

"Honestly, George." She heaved a heavy sigh. "It's not enough. It'll never be enough to get me through the weekend." Tightening her brow, she let worry and pain spill down her cheeks. "How could you?"

"I'm sorry." George's tone was pleading.

"Mom."

She whimpered.

"Mom! We're not gonna do this. We're not freaking out, okay?"

"Well, what am I going to *do? What?* The whole weekend is ruined. *Ruined!*"

I felt panic creeping over the backseat and mingling with hysteria in the front. My father picked an ever-present hangnail on his left thumb while my mother pulled out her rosary and wildly fingered the beads. It didn't take much to whip my parents into a frenzy. I'd seen frustration borne out over a lot less than a nearly empty bottle of much-needed Vicodin: a scrap of Kleenex left on the floor, a bit of scrambled egg caught in the fold of a cotton shirt, a set of curtains left open overnight.

"Mom, here's what we're gonna do. Mom, listen!"

"What!"

"Just settle down, okay? Everything's going to be fine. Dad"—I checked the mirror—"everything will be okay. Mom, when we get to Chrissy and Bill's, take a pill and have a couple glasses of wine, okay? Mix the drugs *and* the alcohol." I laughed the second it came out of my mouth. I laughed, recognizing the slow skid that had made such sideways logic seem like a damn good idea, a stroke of genius. My mother had gone over the handlebars of chronic illness dozens of times, and every time we witnessed it, in slow motion, from the curb. We reached out, but she always managed to slip right through our fingertips. My own grip felt especially slippery. Sure, we helped her clean up the road rash, pick the pebbles out of her palms, but the pain, that was all hers. So, hell yeah, I thought, enough's enough; mix it up.

"Can I do that?" she asked.

"Yes, you can," I said, emphatic. "It'll be fine. Tomorrow morning take another one, and in the meantime we'll dig up a doctor. I'm sure Chrissy and Bill have a few doctor friends. They have drugstores here . . . too . . . Terry." I looked her in the eye. "Just settle. Please."

We found a doctor that night—one of the cousins, of course—and had the problem solved, the prescription picked up, and thus order restored, before heading off to the ordination the next morning. The wheelchair glided down the center aisle of the cathedral as my father pushed, his rubber SAS soles squeaking, step by step, against Italian marble. He parked her in front of the first pew, nearer to the chapel of the Sacred

Heart, built during the Depression as a devotion to a compassionate Jesus who understood the struggles of his people. George and I slid quietly into the first pew so we could keep an eye on her, just in case. I listened to the methodic hiss of her oxygen tank and watched her tremble through a long, slow breath. Then something settled in. The tightness around her jaw disappeared and her cheeks, soft as a baby's behind, fell into an easy repose.

Her eyes, though, had a pristine sparkle like a snow-covered lake on a sunny winter day. Looking back, I can honestly say the look on my mother's face was one I never saw before or after—not at my siblings' weddings, not at the birth of her first grandchild, not when she wrote my last tuition check, not even when the Packers won the Super Bowl. She would have said it was the Holy Spirit. The expression was joyful and excited, sure, but there was something else too, something more serene, like a preparedness that came from a lifetime of practiced trust.

As a sea of some 250 clergy worked its way down the aisle through a cloud of incense, chasubles flowing, birettas perched, my father leaned over with a wry smile and whispered in my ear, "Lots of hocus-pocus today."

My shoulders shook under a silent, fitful church laugh, until eventually the laughter gave way to longing. I longed for her kind of faith—the unassuming, rock-solid faith that took a lifetime to build yet seemed so effortless—the kind of faith I prayed for.

14

Assisi

My niece Betsy and I ran a marathon in Rome today, Sunday, March 23, 2003. We ran past the Vatican, St. Peter's, JP II saying Mass, past the Spanish Steps and the Trevi Fountain. Twenty-six-point-two miles, and don't forget the .2.

That .2, it's ugly.

It took me exactly two hours, 247 minutes. I think I left my uterus at mile twenty-two, right there on the Piazza Navona. I'm not so sure my mother was watching over me from above that day. Running was never her thing. We missed Mass. George thought I was dead. He cried when I crossed the finish line. I forgot to tell him how slowly I ran. Betsy ran faster. She's twenty-two, fresh, young, and tiny, like a cocktail bun. She doesn't drink or smoke. She's the hare, I'm the tortoise. The Kenyans won; they got all the half bananas.

There was no thrill of victory, no agony of defeat. No emotion that clearly defined. No, the feeling was somewhere in the middle where real life takes place, where thrills and agonies look an awful lot alike.

It's so out of character, running.

WE HAVE JOINERS on this trip too, although fewer than I expected: Amy's husband, Tommy, and their oldest daughter, Abby. Tommy is here on business, buying guns for his invention. His mother died too. Abby is fifteen. Tommy prodded her into running the five-kilometer portion of the marathon. Our eyes locked when, after only a few hundred feet, they pulled her onto the 5K course, away from me. I saw watery fear ready to spill onto streets she didn't know, in a city she'd never been to.

I knew for a second what it felt like to be a mother, and then she disappeared into the crowd.

How many kilometers in 26.2 miles?

I don't run. Ask anyone. I watch the Lifetime channel's made-for-TV movies.

The marathon was for charity, the American Diabetes Association. A tribute, I suppose, to my nonrunning mother.

Lord.

I MIGHT NEED the money we raised someday, if diabetes, God forbid, comes a knockin'.

It really rolled in after Terry died, the money.

No backing out.
I don't run.

THE ADA SENT a training manual, a schedule, a how-to.
I grabbed a beer and read the whole thing.
Smoke curled into my eye, stinging.
Not one word in the manual about the chafing.
It's ugly.
I don't run. Ask anyone.

SINCE WE RAN past the pope, I'm making it count for Mass. Hell, I'm making it count for a year's worth of masses. George will agree. Our rules are relaxed. There are crumbs in the Wedgwood butter. It's not perfect the way it used to be. It feels like we're all walking through Jell-O.
I'm chafed in some pretty odd places.

GRANDPA TOLD BETSY, "So we missed Mass, let it go." But she didn't, so here we are in Florence, just two days after the 26.2 miles, at Mass in the Medici Chapel, around the corner from our hotel. I wanted to stay in bed.
Lord, help me set a better example.
It's in Italian, but Mass is Mass.
La pace sia con voi. La pace sia con voi. La pace sia con voi. La pace sia con voi. La pace sia con voi.

• • •

MY FATHER SAW them first. That's important.

He elbowed me in the ribs after Communion and gestured with his eyebrows. Five red roses, an odd number, one for each of us who had lost.

A spouse, a parent, a grandparent.

Those roses stood in a porcelain vase perched at the feet of the Blessed Mother.

I will let fall a shower of roses . . . Remember, O most gracious Virgin Mary . . .

He believed. I saw it. You know belief when you see it. It's gone as soon as it comes.

He gasped the beauty and the sorrow.

He cried and prayed.

Grief connects us.

THEY LEFT US in Venice, Tommy and Abby, and flew home. We rented a car and drove south to Assisi, George, Betsy, and I.

DRIVING IS NOT the same in Italy. For starters, the road signs are in Italian. The Autostrada is no place for indecision. The Italians will drive right up your ass and pop you into an olive tree.

The Italians will spend an hour uncorking a bottle of wine, describing its fruity essence, its otherworldly beauty.

And then they'll drive right up your ass.

My father picked his hangnails in the backseat until they bled.

My sweet little Betsy is a shitty navigator. I don't care if the map is in Italian.

WE'RE GOING TO Assisi because my aunt Dorothy, my mom's sister, asked us to go. We're going because my father feeds the birds, and my mother called him St. Francis.

Mom, I'm bringing our St. Francis to Assisi.

We're on a pilgrimage.

Grief connects us.

THE MARATHON HAS left me crippled.

ASSISI IS OTHERWORLDLY, tucked in the hills where the heavens open up, the sun pours forth, the angels sing.

It's ridiculous. St. Francis bottle openers, foam fingers, and snow globes, and enough rosaries to sink a ship or end communism once and for all.

It's a Catholic Disneyland.

WE ARRIVED ON a Sunday. I said, "Where's the bar?" George did too, but Betsy said we had to go to Mass, again. We walked. I smoked Merits outside and waited while Betsy and George asked for directions. A dark-haired American struggled over ancient cobblestones with a jogging stroller. Ridiculous. He pointed to the Basilica of St. Clare and said to his wife, "I think it's right up here." A New Yorker. Then he asked me, "*Dove si trovala basilica?*"

"I don't speak Italian."

"I'm sorry, it's just . . . you look like you belong here."

"Must be my mustache."

Lord, help me be a better example.

TWENTY-SOME CHURCHES, TWO basilicas, three hundred Franciscans, and eight Poor Clares later we finally found Mass.

See what I mean? Catholic Disneyland.

Betsy wept the beauty and the sorrow.

I had nothing to give—no smile, no hug, no touch, no tears, no offering.

Lord, help me. I am crippled.

THE WINE HERE is like manna, otherworldly. George and I drink and Betsy prays. She says she's doing "inner work."

I say, "Inner work, schminner work."

Lord.

IT'S A SACRED destination, the tomb of St. Francis.

He's in there. Dead, but not really. He has a prayer.

People make pilgrimages, kneeling, praying, offering. There are scores of offerings in that tomb. Crutches—sadness, injury, doubt, despair—thrown down.

And a prayer picked up.

Lord, make me an instrument of your peace . . .

WE'RE ON A pilgrimage.

St. Francis delivered a sermon to the birds. There's a picture of it in every hotel room. I wonder, did they listen?

He has a prayer.

Where there is despair, hope.

I CRASHED THE rental car into the side wall in the parking lot of the Grand Hotel Assisi.

My mouth opened and offered a litany of unmentionables.

Our rules are relaxed now.

There are crumbs in the Wedgwood butter. It's not perfect the way it used to be.

It's a sacred destination.

George picked his hangnails in the backseat until they bled.

Lord, make me . . .

15

Church and Brunch

About six months or so after my mother died, I called my father one day and said, "I think I found a Mass you might like." A few weeks earlier, he had declared he was no longer going to regularly attend Sunday Mass. Offering no other explanation, he simply sighed and said, "I've had enough." He had made statements like that before, sweeping and unilateral, but they usually had to do with lemon drop martinis and dogmatic dinner guests with lipstick on their teeth. This, however, was another story.

I always knew he saw Catholicism differently than most, certainly differently from my mother, but it never occurred to me that he would shrug off its most basic practice in her absence. The decision made sense, though. I felt his reasons somewhere in my soul and knew he was right. I was actually a little jealous—Mass was a painful experience with my mother gone. Still, her words, "Keep an eye on Daddy," echoed around the hollow place she had left in my heart. I knew he was wrong too. For once, hindsight stepped up and behaved. It pulled out a crimson Sharpie, no less, and drew me a picture; a line, crisscrossing around the past and into the present, revealing a series of tight little over-lapping circles, intersecting over the dots of his skepticism and those of her conviction. It was a tangled mess, for sure, but one without the other, doubt without certainty, pulled the line straight and onto a disturbingly empty page.

"You did, did you?" he replied. I heard his smirk through the phone.

"Yeah, I think you'll really like the priest. I met him at a dinner party at Gerry Steele's the other night. He seems like a really good guy." Frustration with stiff, uninspired priests had been another of George's issues with the church. I sensed this priest was different, spirited, so I asked my friend Gerry and her husband Chris to throw a small dinner party and give me a chance to interview him.

"Really?" George was playing me, using the parental "we'll see" tone, the one parents use when they have no intention of "seeing" at all.

"Yeah, I thought maybe we could go out to brunch after. You pick the place. I might even let you pay."

"Is that so?" He chuckled. I knew I had him. My father enjoyed picking up the tab almost as much as he enjoyed eating. Food was the easiest way in. The rest was in God's hands.

"Maybe. We'll see." It meant something different when I said it.

The following Sunday I heard him coming up the stairs as I stood at the bathroom sink brushing my teeth. I lived in a two-bedroom apartment in a redbrick four-family on Henry Clay in Whitefish Bay, just a few blocks from the Inn. He paused at the door. I stopped brushing and listened. Knock, knock . . . knock, knock, knock . . . knock, knock. (Shave and a haircut, two bits.) I smiled at his signature rhythm and headed for the door.

"Good morning," he said with a grin.

"Hey, hang on a sec. I'm almost ready. The paper's over there," I said, motioning to the ottoman.

"Thanks." He grabbed a handful of peanut M&M's I kept in a bowl on the bookshelf near the door, shook them in his hand like dice, settled into an oversize chair, and leafed through the paper. He looked good—white oxford shirt, tan cotton sweater, and khaki pants. Not exactly *GQ* but put together. For fifty years he had let my mother, and us, believe he was a color-blind fashion illiterate. Every morning he'd walk out of their bedroom looking like a prison escapee who had just pilfered the racks at Jos. A. Bank. The charade, at least where it concerned going out in public, ended abruptly at her wake. I guess it just didn't make sense anymore.

"Is it nice out?"

"Oh, it's gorgeous, just *gorgeous.*"

"Where should we go for brunch?"

"I don't know. I brought my folder."

My father kept file folders full of information having to do with . . . anything, really, but mostly food: newspaper clippings, magazine articles, recipes, photos, and sometime crumbs. They were kept, in alphabetical order, in a cheap wooden filing cabinet in the garage, each one marked neatly with black Sharpie—Anchovies, Asparagus, Beer, Brunch, Brussels Sprouts, Cabbage, Gravy, Ham, Osso Buco, Tenderloin Tips—you name it. He was like Ready Reference. We could call him up any time and ask, for instance, "Hey, Dad, do you have a file on tea?"

To which he'd reply, "I don't know, let me check."

We'd wait patiently on the line until he came back. And sure enough, he had a file on tea. "Well, I'll be damned," he'd say. "Whaddya know?"

"Ready?" I asked, grabbing my keys.

"Yep."

"Where's your folder?"

"It's in the car."

"Wanna grab it and I'll pull my car around?" I drove. We had an understanding. If I were shot, or perhaps having a heart attack, and help was nowhere to be found, then maybe I'd let him drive. But only then.

"Okeydokey."

He was right. It was a gorgeous day. The warm air was perfumed with spring—daffodils, tulips, and bluebells—and the grass, littered with dandelions, had managed to turn green overnight. Wisconsin winters step aside for spring every year, yet somehow it's always a delightful surprise.

He stood in the street, about a block and a half west of the lot behind my building, leaning against my mother's Buick, wearing a pair of prescription sunglasses that he had picked up, I believe, during the Carter administration. They had a milk chocolate tint and round plastic rims that were too big for his face, a look that on anyone else might have seemed purposeful, even stylish, but on him just looked ridiculous. He didn't "do" style, in the fashion sense of the word, on purpose. If it caught up with him at all, it was either by chance or on Father's Day, wrapped in a box with a bow. Since he didn't believe in replacing things that were not broken, time passed and sometimes style circled back around and found him again, but it was rare. The shades hadn't quite made the trip.

After five minutes of his fiddling around with the seat belt, I finally buckled him in. *THE GREATEST GENERATION CONQUERS GERMANY AND JAPAN BUT IS BESTED BY VCRS AND SEAT BELTS.* Seriously. He settled into the passenger's seat and tossed his brunch folder, a book, and his regular glasses on the dash.

"That's not gonna stay."

"What?"

"That stuff on the dash."

"Sure it will."

"I don't think so."

"We'll see."

I pulled away and all his stuff slid onto the floor. He tried to fold himself in half and set it up, but the seat belt had him in its grip. "I got it," he grunted.

"Dad, just leave it. We'll get it when we park."

"Nope, no . . . I've got . . . it." He pinched the folder between his thumb and forefinger, pulled it onto his lap, and flipped it open. "So, what do you think?"

"I don't know," I said, peeking over at the pile. "What are our choices?"

"Let's see . . ." He leafed through what must have been fifty loose pages of advertisements, magazine articles, and restaurant reviews, skipping everything that read "upscale" because he didn't like the word. Its overuse offended him. "How can *every* place be upscale?" he would ask. "What does that even mean?" He felt the same way about "in-depth" reporting. "If *all* news coverage is 'in-depth' now, what was it before?" He had a point.

We ended up choosing Miss Katie's diner. He

came across an advertisement and I said I had never been there. A little slice of Milwaukee local color, and not what you'd call upscale, Miss Katie's fit the basic criteria. The ad said it had a full bar too, which didn't hurt.

My father liked to read books before, and sometimes during, Mass, a practice most folks give up shortly before their First Holy Communion. We were not allowed to have books in church, or Cheerios or apple juice, or anything else. We had to sit quietly and pray. George, on the other hand, had his own set of rules. He brought books to church somewhat religiously, if you'll pardon the pun. For the most part they contained some religious word or idea in the title, like *pope* or *Christianity* or maybe even *Jesus,* so they appeared as if they were appropriate pre-Mass reading, but the content was rarely in lockstep with church teachings.

"What's the book?" I asked, as we walked along the chipped sidewalk toward the front of St. Rita's.

He held it up in the sunlight: *Is the Pope Catholic? A Woman Confronts Her Church.* See what I mean?

I cocked my head, covering my brow with my hand, squinted at him, and laughed. Like I said, the rest was in God's hands.

As we mounted the steps, I saw George admiring the church. Just a few months earlier, the two of us stood together on a dusty Roman street, eating gelato, our unified gaze fixed on an imposing Vatican wall. There is nothing imposing about St. Rita's. It's a simple redbrick building tucked on the corner of Cass and Pleasant, just south of Brady Street, on Milwaukee's east side. There is no steeple to be seen from afar, just a subtle stone cross at the center of the roof. Named for St. Rita of Cascia, patroness of impossible cases, it's the kind of church a person might drive right past and never notice. George's stride was comfortable. He casually held the door for me, as if we were entering my house or his.

Inside, however, it is unmistakably a Catholic church, beautiful, but in an understated kind of way. We took a kneeler in a pew on the left, toward the front. I leaned forward, set my elbows on the seat back in front of us, put my face in my hands, and started to say a Memorare. *Remember, O most gracious Virgin Mary.* My father shifted. *That never was it known that . . .* He shifted again. I looked over and saw him pull one hearing aid from a tiny black leather purse in his pants pocket, stick it in his right ear, and crank it on and off with his fingernail. Each twist of his finger caused it to let out a high-pitched peal that resonated in my fillings like a foil gum wrapper.

"What are you *doing?*" I asked.

"I can't get"—crank—"this thing to work."

"It's making a noise."

"It is?"

"Yes. You can't hear it?"

"No. It's noisy in here."

He was right. The atmosphere hummed with excited chatter, different from the typical peaceful pre-Mass hush we were used to. I slid across the smooth wood and sat back. People greeted each other with hearty hellos, hugs, and kisses on both cheeks. On the walls surrounding the nave, paintings of St. Francis, St. Rita, St. Thérèse, and a few other saints I should know but don't, watched and listened.

I reached over to tuck his sweater tag in and noticed he was still wearing his sunglasses. "What's going on there?" I asked, nodding toward his face.

"Where?"

"Your sunglasses."

He reached up, pulled them off, and put them back on.

"Are you gonna wear those through the whole Mass?"

"I left my other ones in the car." He grinned.

"You're not gonna go get them, are you?"

"Nope."

"Do you want me to get them?"

"Nope."

Apparently, the escapee routine was not completely dead.

"Do you think you look like Jackie Onassis in those?"

Smile. Twitch.

Some things you just have to let go.

"I think you're really going to like this priest."

"Think so?"

"Yeah. His name is Father Tim. Last week he was excellent." Then I added, "They call him 'Father What a Shame.'"

"I don't get it."

"As in, what a shame he decided to become a priest instead of getting married."

"I still don't get it."

"Because he's kind of a dish, Dad."

Smile. Twitch.

As I said, my mother was the keeper of the keys in the faith department. She opened the doors and showed us the way. She was our spiritual bus driver, and since she had died, Mass felt like nothing but a brutal crash of emotions, insides broken in a million tiny pieces, colliding with outsides that were trying desperately to look put together. Honestly, for a while I could hardly stand it. Her presence at Mass was so overwhelming, every time, that it pulled a surge of tears from my gut and sent them pouring over my cheeks into my nose, my mouth, and the sleeve of my sweater. It was ugly, or maybe it was beautiful. I don't know.

Mass is ritual and practice, which on some

days brings memories and tears. On others, it means having an opportunity to plan your week, iron out your grocery list, or ponder your golf swing. Something about the way Father Tim says Mass lets you feel good either way. He's less piety and more humanity. Yet he has a fervent energy that is truly dazzling. His Mass leaves you with an amazing feeling of enthusiasm and wonder. He's gifted in a very Christ-like way. He feigns vanity, but his message is one of humility, reverence, inclusiveness, and trust.

He stood among us that day, in the center aisle, wearing a gold chasuble. I wondered what he thought when he glanced over at George, whose sunglasses made him look like Anne Bancroft did playing Annie Sullivan in *The Miracle Worker*. Even under the shades I could tell George was paying attention. He sat unusually still, with his hands folded quietly in his lap. He had finally left his hangnails alone.

Jesus, I trust in you. That was the message of the homily. It was simple, one that George and I had heard and forgotten dozens of times over the years. Father Tim invited the congregation to say it out loud, "Jesus, I trust in you," three times. And with that, my father glanced over at me, wearing a satisfied little grin, and gave me a tender nod. I could see a sprinkle of mist on his cheeks, and I knew that certainty had gained ground on doubt. The nod, though, that's what stuck with me. It changed the ritual I had known my entire life. My father looked at ease in a way I hadn't seen since Terry had died—maybe not ever—like he had parked a truckload of grief with Jesus and trusted that he would know how to help unload it.

George took my hand as we began the Our Father. This, too, we had done as a matter of ritual hundreds of times, but that day we folded our hands around that nod. His hand was rippled with veins, knobby, and coarse like the bark of a weathered maple, and his grip was gently strong. He pressed his thumb softly into the back of my hand. I looked down and smiled at the deep gray groove that ran along the center of the nail. A birthmark of sorts, that groove had grown more pronounced after two unfortunate meetings with the band saw at the restaurant. As a kid I used to run my small fingers along it, back and forth, back and forth. I didn't know him without it.

We held hands like that until the sign of peace; then he wrapped his arms around me in a tight embrace and said, "Peace, Julie. I love you."

"I love you too, Dad."

The crush of tears finally came as we exited the pew for Communion. My father stepped back, laid an almost imperceptible hand on my shoulder, and pressed me ahead of him. He did this all the time, of course, in deference to my mother or any other woman who happened to be behind him. It was a tiny maneuver, sure, one you don't see all that often anymore, one I was actually quite accustomed to, but it set me off. I felt fat tears roll one after another over my eyelids and down my cheeks, and I watched them drop onto the tips of my dusty loafers. I suppose I had my own truckload to drop off. I missed Terry as much as he did, maybe even more. She did give birth to me, after all. It's ugly, though, that cry when you're on your way to Communion. There's nowhere to hide. But still, you go.

We came around, slipped back into the pew, set the kneeler on the floor, and slid forward in unison. I put my face in my hands and started a Memorare. *Remember, O most gracious Virgin Mary . . .* Again, George shifted. *That never was it known that anyone who fled to your protection, implored your help, or . . .* Shift. I waited for the ping of the hearing aid, but it didn't come. Instead, he tapped me on the shoulder and handed me a hankie. I took it without a word and pressed it to my nose. It smelled pretty, like Shalimar. It took me a second to realize what he had done. I looked up at the Madonna and Child statue over the pulpit and saw in my mind's eye George and Terry's bathroom and the gold-trimmed oval mirror where my mother kept her powder and her perfume. I knew it was still there. I knew it hadn't been touched. And I saw him pick up the glass bottle, remove the sapphire lid, hold his hankie aloft, and spray it with a delicate whisper of a reminder. It was beautiful.

GOD, IT SEEMED, had done his job. It was time for me to do mine. So after Mass, as planned, we headed over to Miss Katie's. It smelled like you want a diner to smell, like a deliciously greasy pile of hash browns, bacon, and sausage. A cloud of cigarette smoke hung in the doorway between the bar and the dining area. George and I slid into a mint green vinyl booth near the window, with a view of the freeway.

"That Father Tim is a real dynamo," George said, folding his place mat up an inch from the bottom and laying down a firm crease.

"I know," I said, relieved. "Did I tell ya?"

"Really, the guy is just superb, *superb.*"

"So," I asked, pressing my luck, "should we make this a habit?"

"Absolutely. Where should we eat next week?"

That was it. We ate and enjoyed. He had the corned beef hash and a pinkish Bloody Mary, and I had two eggs over easy, sausage, toast, and hash browns. When we finished, George lifted his glass, shook the remnants of his drink, and said, "Remind me next week to just get a bottle of beer with breakfast."

And so our new Sunday morning tradition began, drawing strength from the presence of God and each other: Jesus, with brunch and a beer chaser. Much like our dinners at the restaurant show in Chicago, it grew. The college kids came first: Alison and Charlie, my niece and nephew who attended Marquette University. Then there were others: Treasie and the kids, Zach, Conor, Jenny, and Carly; Jeremiah and his wife, Ashley; our cousin Pammy and her husband Tom. The faces varied, the numbers fluctuated, and the eateries shifted along the path to a perfect Bloody Mary, but the routine, both gentle and powerful, remained the same and tapped the familiar intimacy that came with breaking bread.

I suppose, at the time, I sensed it. As George knocked on my door each Sunday, and sat in my chair with the newspaper and a handful of M&M's, he was just seasoning our ritual with characteristically nonexistent pomp. He was the same guy I had met my first day working the brunch but with a softer twitch and quieter tongs. He laughed at me for leaving my vacuum cleaner in the middle of the living room floor three weeks in a row. I told him to mind his own business. He clipped articles from the morning paper about people who were pulled over for driving too slowly and kids who spent eight years in college, bleeding their parents' checkbooks dry. He read while I drove and we laughed until we cried.

Once he brought a mayonnaise jar, intending to

fill it with holy water for his font at the back door.

"What's that?" I asked, watching it roll around on the floor and bump into his shoes.

"That's Mom's holy water jar."

"Lemme see it."

He leaned over and scooped it up. It was an extralarge jar, the kind found in the basement of the restaurant. The label had been soaked off and "someone" had stuck a piece of masking tape across the middle and written "Holy Water" on it with a black Sharpie.

"That is *not* Mom's."

"It sure is," he insisted.

"Dad, Mom kept her holy water in petite plastic jars with pictures of saints and shrines on them. There is no way she ever lugged that thing into church."

"It most certainly is hers."

I looked ahead and let it go. These moments, I realized, filled a hungry hole for each of us. And we lapped them up, both bitter and sweet.

16

Three Days

I'm driving back from a sales meeting in Baraboo, Wisconsin. It's a Thursday in February 2007. I'm on I-94, east of Madison. The road is frozen, full of potholes, and surrounded by brittle, barren fields. The sun's behind a gray curtain of dry clouds. I pick up my cell phone and dial the catering office where Katie works.

She says, "Dad has prostate cancer."

IN A MOVIE there'd be no sound. In real life there's a whir and a cadence, tires on concrete, where a heartbeat used to be. In real life Emmylou Harris is coming out of the speakers. She's lost unto this world.

In a movie there'd be a montage. George smiling and twisting his shaving brush around a chipped coffee cup full of remnants of old soap and lathering his face. George smiling and slapping his naked belly on his way down the stairs. George smiling as he ties his bow tie.

In real life there's noise and silence, silence and noise, a thousand conversations that all mean the same thing, noise that changes nothing. There's a silent, brain-rattling scream.

The earth has gone crooked, like it's trying to shuck me off its edge. It won't have me.

They tell us three to five years.

I pick my hangnails until they bleed.

It's survivable, but I know he's going to die.

There's no room for sameness anymore.

KATIE AND I took him to the doctor.

He lost twenty pounds.

"Keep an eye on Daddy."

They tell us three to five years.

He gets female hormones; we call him Georgia.

They tell us eighteen months.

I PICK MY hangnails until they bleed.

I know he's going to die.

"Keep an eye on Daddy."

He reads.

The future is so noisy. I want to find a corner, curl up, and cover my ears. Instead, I beg and plead against the inevitable. *Jesus, please.* I scratch, claw, and punch my way into peace, into quiet. It doesn't work. I don't trust, so I round-house my way in, kicking and screaming.

Peace won't have me.

MY FATHER IS lonely. I had no idea.

He prays his broken rosary.

He eats canned peaches like they're going out of style.

It doesn't work, him being skinny.
He's not the same anymore.
There's no room for sameness.
I know he's going to die.

"DAD HAS PROSTATE cancer."
They tell us eighteen months.
"Keep an eye on Daddy."
I pick my hangnails until they bleed.
He prays his broken rosary.
I know he's going to die.
Peace won't have me.

ON NEW YEAR'S Eve, I rolled my father a joint on my Pottery Barn coffee table. He always wanted to try marijuana. He talked and talked about legalization. He quoted articles. He dug up statistics.

He turned eighty, so I figured what the hell.

It took forever. I don't roll joints.

I waited until after Mass the next day and gave it to him as he sat down to read the paper. We don't go out for brunch on New Year's Day. That was just thirteen months ago. Today is different.

Today is another day.

Today is June 4, 2007.

"YOU'RE DYING, DAD," I say, three and a half words that taste like bile, slipping across the back of my throat, over my tongue.

These words are waves, charged with an impossible current, churning with the future. There for us to see, to wonder about, but not to mention.

The medication isn't working.

He's sitting across from me on the big flowered chair.

He has his hands on his knees.

He chokes with me, for me, on those words.

"You're dying, Dad."

Today is another day.

HE'S BEEN PUTTING things off—books, nights out, vacations . . . life.

The future is charged, wound tight with noise, waiting.

Next year will never come. Next year just disappeared, perhaps also Thanksgiving and Christmas.

I tell him we need to talk. He says, "Uh-oh." He knows my tone the same way I know his.

He's sitting across from me with his hands on his knees.

Between us—the Pottery Barn table, an ottoman, and three and a half words.

Today is different.

Today is another day.

HE NEVER SMOKED the joint.

He asked, "What is that?"

I replied, "It's marijuana, Dad. You've always said you wanted to try it, so here you go. A gift to celebrate your eightieth year. Let's give it a whirl."

He laughed at me.

"Thanks. I can't," he said.

And I tossed it on the Pottery Barn table.

TODAY IS DIFFERENT.

"The doctor said the medicine isn't working, Dad. You know what that means, right?"

What that means softened his expression, his almond eyes and pink cheeks.

I couldn't tell if it was good or bad, relief or shock, the thrill or the agony.

I still don't know.

REALITY TASTES LIKE bile too, or poison. I am the siren beyond the waves, beckoning him to crash on the rocks of knowledge and truth, of the future.

"I'm not sure," he said.

"It means there isn't going to be a next year."

I feel like I just killed him. Hastening the process with the poison of reality. Crashing hope on the rocks. I'll always wonder.

THE MUTED TV buzzed.

"Today is the day, Dad. *Today* you have fun, not tomorrow."

His time has been cut short. Now he knows.

And now I wonder what I've done.

We can know too many things. There's so much to know, so many truths with sharp edges and fangs and tongues that spit cancer.

I cried.

Now he knows.

I'm a baby, I'm *his* baby, and his friend.

Three and a half words between friends.

TODAY IS DIFFERENT.

That joint sat on the Pottery Barn table while we ate New Year's Day brunch. I cooked. Scrambled eggs, bacon, strawberries, toast.

He nodded toward it and said, "That's a terrible-looking cigarette."

I remember being offended.

"How would you know?"

It took forever. I don't roll joints.

"It looks terrible."

I picked it up and tossed it in the back of my freezer, behind the English muffins and the black bananas.

TODAY IS ANOTHER day.

He's sitting across from me with his hands on his knees.

That joint is still in the freezer.

You're dying, Dad. Three and a half words.

Next year just disappeared.

My father is lonely.

I'm sorry to be the one to tell you. I'm sorry. I'm sorry. I'm sorry.

I cried.

He didn't.

He stood up and opened his arms. I felt them wrap tightly around me, his strong arms of knowledge and truth, of the future.

"Thank you," he said. "Now I know. Thank you. Thank you."

17

Swedish Fish

It's funny how things work out, how a short conversation—on the phone, over a cup of coffee, or during a round of golf, at just the right time—can alter your circumstances and leave a lasting mark. My brother Stevie's wife, Sally, and I had just finished playing nine holes at Squires Golf Club in Port Washington, a pretty, public course twenty minutes north of Milwaukee on the shores of Lake Michigan. The cleats on our shoes clicked in time across the asphalt as we walked toward the car. It was a beautiful day, sunny and warm but not too hot. A soft breeze rolled off the water and rippled through the hawthorn flowers and the fairway grass. It was the end of July. The dog-day warmth had finally melted into the air and the cicadas hummed with delight.

"That was a good round," Sally said, lifting the back door of her minivan. "You played well."

"You think?"

"Sure," she said, her tone unconvincing.

"Thanks." I laughed, and tossed my bag in the car. On the golf course, I had a gorilla-like finesse. My short game, unfortunately, looked exactly like my long game, so I spent most days hacking my way out of the long grass, back and forth over the green. Still, golf agreed with me. I had a penchant for sports that combined physical activity with drinking beer and long periods of rest. Thankfully, so did Sally.

She kicked off her right shoe, and then her left, over the bumper and in between our bags, and said, "Should we get a beer?"

"Yeah. A quick one, though. I want to stop by my dad's this afternoon." I talked to him almost every day, but his cancer had left me with an overwhelming need to lay eyes on him.

"Where should we go?"

"Doesn't matter. You pick."

We ended up at a little steak-sandwich-and-haystack-onion-rings supper club outside of Port Washington. It was the kind of place that had a dusty wreath of plastic flowers hanging from the ladies' room door and a glass jar of Slim Jims behind the bar. The place had a thick, sweet smell, like Murphy Oil Soap. The aroma wrapped itself around me as we made our way through the foyer. A perfect row of empty green vinyl stools lined the bar, so we took seats in the middle and each ordered a Miller Lite.

"So," Sally said, "how do you think your dad's doing?"

I shook my head. "I'm not sure. He seems like he's hanging in there okay."

"Have you ever thought about moving in with him?"

I had considered it. Twice. The first time had been a couple of days after my mother died. I found him and my sister Chrissy sitting in their pajamas at the kitchen table, drinking coffee. Chrissy pulled a brittle rubber band off Terry's black prayer book and began leafing through the holy cards. I sat down across from my father and watched him separate the novenas from the Mass cards. After a very brief discussion about what to do, we set the novenas aside, figuring we might need them someday, slipped the Mass cards back into the battered prayer book, and agreed to bury the book with her. If a person can truly possess a thing, that prayer book was absolutely hers, and its contents were as much, perhaps even more, a part of her soul as any of us. And those cards marked the lives, and deaths, of grandparents, parents, aunts, uncles, cousins, friends, and children of friends. They, we decided, should go with her. *They,* it occurred to me, were already there. And for a second, my heart ached with envy.

As Chrissy carefully wrapped the rubber band back around the book, George looked at me and said, very matter-of-factly, "I know you've been thinking of getting a place of your own. You are more than welcome to move in with me if you want."

He was right. Katie and I had been living and working together for seven years, and while the situation worked, it was time for me to put my big-girl pants on and get my own apartment. Moving in with my father would have defeated the purpose, *and* I would be moving in with my dad.

"Dad . . ."

"Maybe save a little money."

I actually bristled. In my tiny, selfish mind, the notion of moving back in with my parents—or parent, as it were—at thirty-two and single, screamed *spinster*. I'd be just a hip replacement away from a house full of unkempt cats, dirty afghans, and wearing slacks ordered from the back of *Parade* magazine.

"Dad, I can't. I appreciate the offer, really, but I need to figure out a way to be on my *own* for a while, to be . . . responsible for *myself*." Honestly, what an idiot.

• • •

"YEAH," I SAID to Sally, eyeing the row of clocks above the bar. "It's funny you ask. I was thinking about maybe moving in with him just the other day." I took a swig of my beer. It was 4 a.m. in Tokyo.

"Why don't you?" Sally asked.

"It was just a thought, in and out, you know? We were on our way to Mass and he seemed kind of . . . I don't know . . . lonely."

"I think you should."

"You think he'd want me to?"

"Maybe."

"Maybe," I said, but I knew it was a good idea.

A COUPLE OF hours later I found myself on George's patio. He sat across from me, half in the sun and half under the shade of the table umbrella. There was still a fullness in his cheeks, but his skin had become jaundiced. Other than aspirin, and even those he crushed on the counter and stuffed in a banana, I had never witnessed my father taking any medication, over the counter or otherwise. His liver happily opened the door for gin and brandy, it knew how to entertain beer and wine, but medication and cancer—they were the unwanted party crashers. His white undershirt hung loosely around his neck, his comfy, round belly was all but gone, and his gray sweatpants sagged around his slippers and brushed the bricks on the patio. Still, he seemed more of himself. His "George-ness" had somehow grown larger.

He squinted and smiled unconsciously as he slipped his gold opener along the length of a letter that had arrived in the mail. I had watched him do this ten thousand times, at the kitchen or the dining room table, or there on the patio, always with a drink and a happy grin. My father loved opening the mail. He was meticulous about how he did it. Junk went into the garbage can sitting next to his chair. Bills were carefully placed in a "to be paid" folder so they could "be paid" later. All solicitations for charitable donations went in a separate pile and later into an empty tomato box that he sorted through each January. He did all his giving at once, keeping track with a notebook and a chart, so he could weed out the multiples. I looked at the pile of requests and wondered whether, come January, he'd be writing out checks, or I'd be throwing them away.

"Um . . . Dad?" Still figuring out how to spin the conversation without offending his sense of self or calling into question his capabilities, I tried to tread lightly.

"Yeah," he said, not looking up.

"I had a thought."

"Really? Amazing." He smirked.

"Funny."

"What is it?"

"Hypothetically, how would you feel about me moving in here? I mean . . . I've been thinking about moving anyway . . . and I just thought . . ."

His smirk disappeared, his face slackened, and he let out a deep, doglike sigh. He closed his eyes, bit both lips, and cocked his head just a fraction to the right, letting the sun catch the whole of his face. Above the gutters, strips of pea green paint curled against the shingles. My father took good care of his house. I remember being irritated that the painters, who had done the job just a year earlier, had made such a clumsy and obvious oversight.

"Dad, I'm sorry," I said, backpedaling. "If you don't want me here . . . it's cool. I just got to thinking, and I was chatting with Sally . . ."

He set down his mail and prayerfully pulled his hands over the bridge of his nose. "Thank you, thank you, thank you."

"What does that . . . mean?"

"I have wanted to ask one of you girls to move in here for a long time, but I thought it would be too much of an imposition. I didn't want to put any of you out."

Ugh. I swallowed a lump as big as my fist. "Really?"

"Yes, yes," he said, clapping his hands softly.

I've seen some things that most people would consider beautiful—brilliant sunsets behind the

Golden Gate Bridge, bright orange harvest moons shimmering across Lake Michigan, the sprays at the Cliffs of Moher, Michelangelo's *Pietà*, even Pope John Paul II saying Mass at the Vatican. Not one of these things can touch the breathtakingly pure and absolute expression of relief I saw spread itself across my father's face. That look *was* beauty.

THE PLAN WAS for me to move in at the end of September. I would have two full months to pack and give proper notice to my landlord. Cancer clouded the circumstances—sure, that's what cancer does—but still, I was excited. I had a bunch of little future vignettes rolling around in my head: Packers games, chicken wings, climbing the tower at the Schlitz Audubon Nature Center, boning the Thanksgiving turkey, maybe even a little "George and Julie" book club, Christmas decorations, and Tom & Jerrys. Plus, there were the added bonuses of parking my car in the garage and not having to buy toilet paper.

Though it wasn't planned that way, I ended up moving in on August 17. It was a Friday afternoon. I had just finished my fifth week at my new job and I felt good. The seeds of confidence had rooted themselves in the fact that no one had fired me yet. Happy to have the weekend ahead of me, I picked up the phone as I merged onto the expressway and dialed George's number.

"Hello, Pandl's," he answered.

"Hi, Dad."

"Who's this?"

"Me."

"Who's me?"

"Julie." I rolled my eyes and checked the rearview mirror. It happened every time. We had very similar phone voices, my sisters and me, and neither he nor Terry could ever tell the difference. "Whaddya doin'?"

"Sitting on the patio with Peggy, having a glass of wine."

"How do you feel?"

"Well . . . not the greatest."

"How do you mean?" I asked, turning the radio down.

"Well . . . just kind of achy and blah."

Blah meant fatigue, cancer's crony, the unrelenting and selfish sidekick. Fatigue was the uninvited dinner guest with yellow teeth, dirty fingernails, and earwax that showed up at every party, demanded everyone's undivided attention, and overstayed his welcome. Achy, I knew we could kick out. Blah was tougher. "Hmm . . . have you taken anything?"

"I took a Vico Dan an hour or so ago."

Uh-oh, I thought. *That's a first.* My parents were polar opposites in the prescription drug use department. Despite the fact that his cancer had progressed to his pelvis, his ribs, his spine, and his skull, my father approached narcotics with suspicion, concern, even revulsion, as if all pharmaceuticals were distributed by al-Qaeda. My mother, on the other hand, was a bit of a junkie. She was diabetic, of course, so she had legitimate needs, but she secured prescriptions, usually over the phone, so deftly it was like watching a pickpocket at a carnival.

"You can take another one."

"Are you sure?"

"Yes, Dad, I'm sure. The doctor said one or two every six hours. Remember?"

"I don't know—"

"Dad, you have bone cancer. It's okay to take the pills."

After we hung up, it crossed my mind that I should spend the night with him. It was a little wisp of a thought, scurrying through my plan to meet Katie down on the lakefront at Irish Fest. I'll admit it: I did not want to sleep at George's. My job had me traveling, and I was so looking forward to a night in my own bed. Plus, I had not mentally prepared for the somber implications that came along with staying overnight. Never mind the fact that he didn't have HBO. Still, I stopped at my apartment, ran in, and stuffed a toothbrush, T-shirt, and pajama bottoms in a backpack, just in case.

Looking back, I suspect a little piece of me knew the minute I pulled into the driveway that I wouldn't be leaving. But as I turned off the ignition, I held out hope that within an hour or two I'd find myself under a beer tent, listening to Finbar MacCarthy. He and Peggy were still sitting on the patio, an empty chardonnay bottle between them. The sun had dipped between the branches of the big maple in the front yard, illuminating a small swarm of gnats and bleaching the house in a shaft of light. I tossed my keys on the table, plopped into a cushioned seat, and said, "So . . . what's goin' on?"

"Not much," Peggy said.

George looked fatigued. Chubby sacks, like oysters, had fixed themselves under his eyes. His hair was dry and mousy. While his face was an unnerving shade of yellowish gray, the wine had pinked up his cheeks and his earlobes.

"You don't look too good, Dad."

"Yeah," he said, and shook his head. "I don't know what's the matter with me." Peggy and I exchanged a sideways glance. "The pain just came on all of a sudden . . . in the last day or so."

"Have you eaten anything today?"

"Yeah, as a matter of fact, I had some canned peaches," he said with a hearty smile.

Peggy slapped me on the arm. "The ones from the garage."

I knew those peaches. They had survived three

moves and seven presidents. The dented and rusty cans sat on a shelf in the garage right next to the motor oil and the canned ham my mother had purchased during the Cuban missile crisis.

"Seriously? Dad, those peaches are older than I am."

"They're fine!" he said. "You kids are such babies. How do you think the West was won? Besides, peaches were the only thing that sounded good."

That statement raised a giant red flag. *Everything* sounded good to George, *all* the time. I looked over at Peggy and said, "I think I'll spend the night."

I SAID GOOD night to George and crawled into bed at about ten. The sheets were crisp, cold, and perfumed with fabric softener. I rolled over and stared at the bookshelf across the room. My father had bothered to stock it, alphabetically by author, with books of short stories and poetry. That way, if a guest decided to pick one out and read it, he or she could, in theory, finish it during his or her stay. The bedroom door was slightly ajar, and the light from the hallway cast a shadow along the book jackets, some split and curled with age, some clean and new. In the dark, on the very top shelf, stood the Holy Family: Mary, Joseph, and the baby Jesus, watchful statues placed there by my mother.

240

Over the soft whoosh of the cool air escaping the floor vent, I heard the light humming in the bathroom. I took a deep breath and quietly began to cry. I was overwhelmed. I looked over at the orange plastic backpack I had packed for the night and realized that I had done nothing to prepare for the move. It was too soon. Tears rolled over my cheeks, down my neck, and soaked into my T-shirt. "Okay, Mom," I whispered. "I'm a little annoyed that you're not here, so you've gotta help me. I mean it, Terry, no screwing around. I don't know what to do. Honestly, what should I do? You have to help." Indecision and anxiety pulled me into a fit of hysterical sobs, peppered with occasional whimpers of "Help me, please." It wasn't pretty. Just before I fell asleep, I squinted up at Jesus, Mary, and Joseph and said, "You three could lend a hand here too."

They were still staring at me when I opened my eyes the next morning. The house was quiet, except for the faint but steady drone of my father's sleep apnea machine. He was still asleep. I closed my eyes and realized that I had forgotten to throw my book in my backpack. I had been stuck in the first fifty pages of *Catch-22* for weeks. Reading in bed with a cup of tea was part of my morning routine, a guilty pleasure that gave the day a peaceful start. From the bed I canvassed the bookshelf, hoping to find an appealing short story. And there he was, Joseph

Heller, completely out of place among James Joyce, O. Henry, and Edgar Allen Poe.

When a coincidence occurs, acknowledge it; that's what the writing teachers tell you to do. So I will. At that moment I thought it was luck, and in the next I realized it was neither coincidence nor luck. I slid George's copy of the book off the shelf and blew the dust into the morning air. The crusty jacket cracked as I opened it and thumbed through the yellowed pages. And believe it or not, my mother's Mass card slipped out onto the floor. There she was, St. Thérèse, with her crucifix and her showering bouquet of roses, gazing up at me wisely. Now, I'm not much for signs, but this was a little like being slapped upside the head. I looked up at the Holy Family and said, "I get it. I got it. Nice touch, very subtle." I bent down, picked up the card, flipped it over, and read the verse from Timothy. "I have fought the good fight, I have finished the race, I have kept the faith."

So I padded down the hall, past the wedding and high school graduation pictures, knocked softly on George's door, and walked in. There he was, sound asleep. The machine on the nightstand whirred as it pushed air through the mask on his face. It looked like a jock strap with an oxygen mask. He looked like some kind of slapstick version of Hannibal Lecter in *The Silence of the Lambs.*

"Dad," I whispered, and shook his foot. "Dad." I scanned the empty side of the bed, recalling how every Friday and Saturday night during high school I stood at the foot of that bed and woke them both up. The room smelled like Ammens powder and sherry. *"DAD."*

He bolted upright and pulled off the headgear. "What? What? What's the matter?"

"Whaddya doin'?" I smiled.

Falling back onto his pillows with a gasp, he said, "Nothing, sleeping. What is it?"

I sat on the end of his bed and said, "I'm moving in today, okay? I'm gonna stay here now. I'm not leaving."

"Okeydokey," he said, and fell back asleep.

MY BROTHER STEVIE met me at my apartment and helped me pack up my immediate needs—clothes, toiletries, and books. My comfortable furniture had to wait. On my way back to George's, I stopped at the grocery store and picked up some fresh food and a six-pack of Miller Lite, because I knew he didn't have either. I wasn't about to eat the peaches, and George had a thing about light beer.

At some time during my fifth or sixth year at school, just to see what kind of reaction I'd get, I told him I intended to drop out of Loyola University and attend clown college instead. I had even done a little research and found a very respectable school down in Sarasota, Florida, that seemed to "fit my needs." Completely straight-faced, I expressed my desire to "take the road less traveled" and explore the unique and happy world of rodeos, circus folk, and clowndom. When I finished, he smiled, folded his newspaper, looked me in the eye, and said, "That's fine with me, Julia, whatever you decide." But when he found out I preferred a light beer over a porter, a stout, or even an ale, my father stared into my soul with such bitter disappointment, I actually cried. Other people, of course—friends, neighbors, in-laws, even strangers—anyone other than his own off-spring—could choose whatever they wanted to drink. I watched my father go out of his way, time and time again, to pick up a bottle of Drambuie, or sloe gin, or crème de cacao. Rusty Nail, anyone? Coming right up. Alabama Slammer? Not a problem. How about a nice Pink Squirrel? The liquor bottles are still gathering dust in the basement.

I lugged the groceries through the garage door and into the kitchen and found George still in his pajamas, sitting at the table. "My God, my *God!*" he exclaimed, standing up, slapping one hand to his forehead and gesturing to the bags with the other. "Why did you buy all this food? I've got plenty of—"

"Oh, no. Listen, Georgia." I stood with my

hands on my hips and looked him right in the eye. "I remember what it was like when you were in charge of the fridge, and I'm still scarred from it."

He smiled.

"It's not funny. I'm serious. If I'm living here I'm getting food from a *real* store. I'm not eating whatever two-decade-old science experiment you've got frozen in the garage. Got it?"

"Okay."

"And don't try to sneak in anything you pulled out of the Dumpster at the restaurant." Yes, he had actually done this with a case of pecan halves that had come off the delivery truck infested with some sort of funky insect found only in Texas. They never made it into the restaurant, but they did make it into George's peach cobbler at home. "I mean it."

"All right, all right, you're the boss."

Stevie unpacked my stuff while George and I put away the groceries. Except for a door loaded with twenty years of assorted condiments with crusty lids, a five-pound bag of Maytag bleu cheese, an upside-down bucket of cottage cheese (he flipped cottage cheese after opening it in order to maintain freshness for months beyond the expiration date—it does work), and a bowl of slippery canned peaches, the fridge was empty. I squatted down and began filling the bottom shelf with yogurt.

"What're these?" George asked, holding up a clear plastic container of Swedish Fish.

"Swedish Fish. I'm addicted to those, so get used to them." I had given up peanut M&M's for Lent a few years earlier and quickly became hooked on Swedish Fish. What can I say? I'm weak.

"What are they?"

"It's candy, Dad. You've never heard of them?"

"No," he said, examining the package in the light. George loved candy. As a kid, I remember waking up in the morning, alone in their bed. Their nightstands, both carved oak with a shelf on the bottom, a drawer, and a dusty glass top, matched in style and form but not content. My mother's was home to the telephone, in case somebody called in the middle of the night, a rosary, a prayer book, and a six-inch statue of St. Thérèse, also in case somebody called in the middle of the night. On the flip side, George's was littered with books, Ammens powder, candy wrappers, and piles of half-eaten spearmint leaves, orange slices, and gumdrops.

Candy in our house—I'm talking about the good stuff—was well hidden. You just can't keep candy around with nine kids. The reason, and I'm not sure if it's related to motion or gravity, is one of Newton's laws. I hid my Halloween candy in a cigar box behind my Barbie town house. Terry slipped Hershey bars in the bookshelves among the Russians, Dostoyevsky and Tolstoy, where she figured they were least likely to be discovered. And George stuffed his bags of spearmint leaves and gumdrops in his dresser drawers. The boxes of Russell Stover candy that arrived every Christmas and Easter were the one inert exception. Having ferreted out the caramels, we let the crappy stuff sit on the kitchen counter for weeks. There lay the battered raspberry, orange, and coconut cream remnants, each one stabbed through the bottom with a tooth, a fingernail, or a pen and tossed back among the wrinkled wrappers for the next guy.

"Try a few," I said. "They're kinda like licorice, only seriously more delicious."

He chewed a few into his dental work and raised his eyebrows with delight. "Damn good."

"I told you."

He picked one up and inspected it. "They're like Jub Jubs." That's Jujubes or Jujyfruits, to the normal person. "What are they called?"

"Swedish Fish, Dad," I said, continuing to load the fridge. "I can't believe you don't know what they are."

THAT NIGHT WE watched a preseason Packers game. If memory serves, they played Seattle. George, still in his T-shirt and sweatpants, sat in the blue corduroy mechanical recliner he had purchased, postamputation, for

247

Terry. The thing was broken. It had been since day one. It had buttons to move it up and down. The up arrow, which you would think meant "up," as in "stand up," actually meant "down," as in "recline." And the down arrow, of course, really meant "up," but the button worked only occasionally, so once you were "up" you couldn't get "down." Confusing? Tell me about it. You should have seen George. He sat there, trapped, with his feet up in the air and his finger on the "down" button for the length of the second quarter. Finally, he looked over at me, completely helpless, and said, "Will you get me a couple of those Russian sardines?"

The next day I went to Mass alone. It was jarring, leaving the house without him, like wearing a wool sweater on a boiling hot day. The vacant passenger's seat and the conversation I had with myself offered palpable insight, but the slow twists and turns on Lake Drive were a bit of a tranquilizer. It didn't hit me until I sat on the chilly pew at St. Rita's, slipped my hand in my pocket, and wrapped it around my mother's pyx. The pyx I had grabbed from the untouched dust on top of her jewelry box before I walked out the door. Its roundness was soothing. I popped it open, closed my eyes, and saw my father sitting across from me at Ma Fischer's, just two weeks earlier, pushing pancakes around his plate. I snapped it closed and realized that our church and brunch days were over. I would bring him Communion from then on. I popped it open and snapped it closed, over and over, while the voices around me united and fell into the rhythm of the Mass.

On Monday I skipped work. At 7 a.m., I paced in the driveway, my bare feet picking up pebbles from the cool concrete, and dialed Debbie, my new boss.

"Hello, this is Debbie," she answered.

"Hi, it's Julie."

"Hi."

Having never called in "unable" to work, I had to pull the words out carefully, like a foreign object. "Listen . . . I'm . . . not going to make it in today."

"What's up?"

"I moved in with my dad over the weekend, a little unexpectedly, and he's not doing well. I'm taking him to the doctor today, and we're having the hospice conversation." I felt queasy. "I'm sorry."

"It's okay," she said.

God love her. I sighed.

"We knew this was coming," she offered.

We did?

I made George take me out to lunch before his doctor's appointment. He chose the Whitefish Bay Inn. He looked good. His tan sweater and khaki pants hung around his body like a bathrobe, and he was a little rickety as he slid into the car, but still. He smelled like Old Spice. We sat in the bar at the two-top next to the half-open, half-closed Dutch door. The room was empty except for an old guy with a face like a worn catcher's mitt, sitting tucked away in the corner, nursing a brown drink, a cigarette, and what sounded like Legionnaires' disease.

We ordered Bloody Marys. I watched Dad peruse the menu like a first-timer, as if he had never seen it before, as if he didn't know every ingredient in every recipe. He smiled the same way he smiled when he looked at the mail.

"Whaddya gonna get?" I asked.

"The Denver omelet sandwich."

"That's a weird one for you. No chicken liver sandwich?" Just saying chicken liver sandwich made me gag a little.

"Nope," he said. "I feel like something different. I haven't had a Denver omelet sandwich in years. How 'bout you?"

"Clubhouse."

He laughed. "Do you ever order anything else?"

"It's still the best in town."

The waitress brought our drinks and took our order.

George raised his glass, smiled, and said, "Cheers."

"Cheers."

"What do you call those things again?"

"What do I call what?"

"Danish . . . trout?"

I laughed. "*Swedish Fish,* Dad!"

"Oh." Smile. Twitch.

We sat quietly for a few minutes, comfortable together in silence. I watched him glance around the cozy, dark bar. I don't know what that look was, but there was something behind it—peace, joy, maybe warmth. His eyes glistened as if he were saying hello, or perhaps good-bye, to a very old friend. Eventually, those eyes landed on me.

"Well . . . Julie, what are you thinking?"

"Dad," I said, folding my paper place mat up from the bottom, pressing an even crease, once, twice, three times. "I think we need to ask for hospice today."

"You do," he said, more a statement than a question.

"I do."

Twitch.

"I do, Dad. We all do." We did. The siblings, myself included, had discussed it. Our mother had hospice for exactly fifteen hours. Everyone felt gypped then and scared now. We had barely settled in to having help and had almost missed the boat and let her die in the hospital. With George, sooner rather than later got the vote.

"Hospice can be helpful now."

Twitch. "Okay."

"Okay?"

"Yeah." He raised his glass and smiled again. "Okay, whatever you kids think."

Okay. That was it. I felt lighter, buoyed somehow against the weight of the circumstances. He had handed over his trust then and there. He gave my siblings and me a wonderful gift and paid us a tremendous compliment. Is there a greater act of true love than trust? If there is, I don't know it.

18

Stella

From the very beginning of his illness, we kept a maroon Mead assignment notebook with a yellow Post-it on the cover that read "George's Notebook." Inside we taped the business cards for a slew of doctors—family practice, urologist, hematologist, and oncologist—and we wrote down the number for Kopp's Frozen Custard, just in case. It went wherever he went. It detailed appointments, phone conversations, medications, hormone treatments, and test results. We all scribbled notes. Reading it now, nearly two years later, feels like the slow backward peel of a fresh and deeply rooted scab. They're just words, really, lined up on a page, one after another;

some cold, some messy, others scary, still others funny. Each one is something else, though, a moment, a snapshot, capturing both absolute sadness and perfect joy.

> Prostate / Bones / Ribs / Spine / Skull,
>   Tuesday, Dr. Kerns, 12:00. Careful,
>   weight-bearing areas
> Affairs in order

It was July, a balmy, breezeless day, sometime after the fourth. I was between jobs and mooching off Chrissy and her family. They were vacationing in Oostburg on Lake Michigan. The corn, indeed knee high, stood peacefully still as Chrissy and I drove south toward Milwaukee. The city lapped eagerly against the farmland, a hospital, a Target, and the shell of a soon-to-be Costco. We were meeting George at the bank so he could approve my signature on his checking account. "There will come a day"—that's what I had said to him—"when you're too sick." Chrissy made for the exit ramp and the words rolled around in my mind, until they folded in on themselves and captured his willingness to surrender ownership of such an intimate task.

We found him in the bank lobby, sitting at a broad mahogany desk with a white marble inlay. The clerk across from him wore a navy pinstripe suit and her hair was in a painfully tight-looking bun. George made the introductions and we commenced the rigmarole of authorizing my signature, a process that undoubtedly had CIA origins. As I inked my John Hancock next to thirty-five green SIGN HERE stickers, I waited for bun lady to ask me for blood and urine samples. Seriously, I think it took less time to get the Iran-contra affair under way.

"When we're through here," George said, "I want to show you my safety-deposit box."

"Excellent," I said, not looking up. "Does that mean I get to keep everything in it?" Bun lady, who, despite the fact that my father found me capable, seemed unconvinced as to my worthiness; she let out a flimsy chuckle.

We left Chrissy waiting in the lobby and walked to the vault. The door looked a lot like a door to a prison cell, except cleaner and prettier. It was beautiful, a shiny golden cage with an intricate system of locks, steel-reinforced concrete, and an armed guard protecting boxes full of important documents and valuable stuff. Treasures. George's box had been placed on a table in the middle of the room.

"They keep the key here," he said, holding it up. "You signed for this too."

"Okay."

He slid the key in the hole and lifted the lid. I felt a quiver of anticipation, as if that box contained some sort of miracle drug that would cure cancer *and* eliminate cankles. The pile of papers had a distinct, musty, back-of-the-garage-like smell. I recognized the odor from the old *Gourmet* magazines he had donated to the catering office. George picked carefully through each "document," one by one, lifting it up, examining it, and setting it aside.

"This is Mom's college diploma."

"Thank God you've got *that* locked up."

"This is an old copy of my will. The updated one's at the house."

"I know."

"This is a pen."

"Did you want someone specific to have it?"

"Here's the title to Mom's car."

"Sure, absolutely," I nodded. "Just in case someone steals Mom's car, right? 'Cause those guys are lining up around the block."

He held up another presumably important document, something with words blurred over the notary seal. "I don't know what this is."

"Dad," I said, smiling, feigning disbelief. "Where . . . are . . . the . . . jewels? Where's the cash?"

He laughed.

"C'mon, let's go out to lunch."

We walked across the street to Panera Bread. The place teemed with midday noise—spoons clanging, men and women chatting, kids screaming. We ordered our food and slipped into a booth, George on one side, Chrissy and I on the other. Halfway through his panini he looked at us and said, "You know, girls, I was thinking . . . about the movie *It's a Wonderful Life* the other day. And . . . I realized . . ." He twitched. His eyes suddenly welled up. One quiet tear rolled down his cheek and socked me—both of us, I think—in the stomach. The surrounding noise fell to a dull murmur. "I realized . . . that I *have* had a wonderful life, kids. I really have. I have no complaints. I had a great wife, a great family. I did what I loved. Honestly"—twitch—"what more could I ask for?" He had a happy smile on his face, despite the tear. Chrissy and I just stared at him.

Those words, coming out of anyone else's mouth, no doubt I would have called cornball. But watching my father serenely and unabashedly assess his eighty-one years was so profoundly reassuring that I felt like I was back in my childhood bed with my head on his stomach and my feet on the wall. Go ahead—try sticking that in a safe-deposit box.

8/20/07: Continuous pain med? Hospice??
8/21/07: Fentanyl Patch 12:50, 3 aspirin
        3:30

So my siblings and I, we pulled our shit together. Not long after I moved in with Dad, we figured out that two of us spending the night with George was better than one. I lived there, and when I traveled for work my siblings cycled in and out. The calendar hanging on the fridge had two names scribbled on every day. Within a week, the number of toothbrushes in the glass next to the sink in the guest bathroom grew from one to seven. Somebody—Stevie or Jeremiah, I think—used mine. Starting when we were kids as a passive-aggressive form of torture, the practice of using the other guy's toothbrush eventually became tolerated, even commonplace.

Impending death, just so you know, does not have the ability to kick history to the curb. It can't. And do you want to know why? Because the child in us, not the adult, sits down at the bedside and holds the hand. Sure, we were taller, fatter, grayer-haired, and slightly more mature versions of ourselves, but we were the same kids who had doled out nicknames like Fatty, Witchy, Chubby, Lusky, Loser, and Little Lotta. We were individuals, and we were who we were, but by some miracle we all landed on the same page where George was concerned. We all understood, I think, that our future held no parents, so we let the past stay where it belonged.

In the beginning, Stevie stayed at the house a lot. We nicknamed him the A-Team, mostly because he displayed kind, gentle, hospice-nurse-like qualities, but also because he had inherited 90 percent of the family's patience genes. The other 10 percent went to Johnny, Jimmy, Katie, Peggy, Chrissy, Amy, and Jeremiah. I did not get any.

I came home late from work one night and the house was dark, inside and out. I thought maybe Stevie had taken George out, but as soon as I got out of my car, I heard the TV. It sounded like a tank battalion rolling through the kitchen and out the back door. The volume on my father's television went as high as sixty-four, and that's where he liked it. Translate that into decibels, and it's something like turning on a leaf blower and sticking it in a crib with an infant.

The two of them, George in his chair and Stevie on the couch, sat mesmerized in the glow of the screen.

"WHAT ARE YOU WATCHING?" I shouted.

George shushed me, a little irritated.

"CAN YOU PAUSE IT FOR A SEC?"

Morphine had made the Pause and Mute buttons a little tricky to find. He stared at the remote with his finger at the ready for a good thirty seconds before finding the button. I glanced at the screen and saw a blurry black-and-white army of Nazi storm troopers stuck in mid–goose step.

"What the hell is this?" I asked.

"It's about the war," George said.

"I'm not sure it's loud enough."

"Dad wants to watch *all* his movies," Stevie said. He smiled and took a swig of a Stella Artois.

George didn't do movies, not like normal people anyway. First off, in terms of ability to operate the VCR, the thing might as well have been the space shuttle, and never mind the DVD player. When I was in college, on Friday nights the phone in my dorm room would ring, and before I could say hello, he'd say, "Okay, I've got the tape in, I pressed Play, and nothing's happening."

"Is the TV on channel three?"

"Oh . . . okay . . . there it goes." Then he'd hang up.

Second, and you'll have to pardon the expression, his movie collection sucked. He was a book guy and a bit of a snob when it came to films. To him, TV was ridiculous, asinine, and an insult to our intelligence. The two exceptions were games featuring the Packers and *Seinfeld.* Go figure. And he learned about movies while reading things like the *National Catholic Reporter*, *Mother Jones*, and the *Progressive.* Consequently, most of his selections remained wrapped in cellophane and consisted primarily of religiously and politically slanted historical dramas about people hardly anybody had heard of—guys like Alexander Nevsky and Andrei Rublev. They were great fun to watch if your other option was, say, prepping for a colonoscopy.

I rolled my eyes and said, "I'm getting ready for bed."

An hour or so later Stevie brought George back to his room, and the two of us tucked him in for the night. After positioning his body neatly under the covers, and his hands in a casketlike fold, he looked up at both of us with weird, wide-eyed excitement and said, "Well . . . I think tonight's the night, kids. I really . . . think it is."

There was something hysterically comforting about his preparedness. Neither Stevie nor I could help but laugh at his let's-get-this-show-on-the-road mentality.

"Dad," I said, "if you can *say* 'tonight's the night,' tonight is probably not going to be *the* night. But just in case it is . . . I love you."

"I love you too. I love you kids."

"I love you too, Dad," Stevie answered.

At three in the morning we both heard him calling for us. Climbing out of bed and hurrying to his room, I wondered if perhaps he had been right. *Maybe it is the night. Maybe this is it.* The open door pitched a wide swath of light from the hallway across his body. His eyes were like saucers, his face paralyzed with terror.

I reached for his hand. "Dad, what's the matter?"

"Kids," he whispered quietly, petrified, "evil's coming to town."

"What?" Stevie asked.

"Evil . . . kids. Evil's coming to town. Evil's coming to town. Evil's—"

"Dad!" I shook his arm. "Wake up. You're dreaming. Wake up." Still, I glanced over my shoulder, half expecting to see the kid from *The Omen* standing in the pitch black frame of the closet door.

"Evil's coming to town."

"Dad," Stevie said, rubbing George's leg, "it's okay. It was just a dream. It's fine."

"Don't leave, kids."

"We're not," we replied in unison.

"We're not going anywhere," I told him.

"I don't want to be alone." He pulled his comforter over his chest.

"You're not, Dad." Again in unison.

"You're not going to be alone ever again," Stevie said.

We pulled up chairs and sat next to him until he fell asleep, neither of us saying a word.

At 6 a.m., Stevie and I met in the kitchen. I was making a pot of tea. He came around the corner in his boxers, his hair a slick, tangled mess. He stopped and stared at me.

"Know what'll scare the shit out of you?"

He smiled.

"When your dying father tells you 'Evil's coming to town' in the middle of the night."

He scratched his head. "Think it was the movie?"

"Ya think?"

9/3, 6:00 a.m.: 1 morphine, 1 antinausea
  pill
11:00 a.m.: 1 morphine, 2 sennas
3:45: 1 morphine, 1 antinausea
Stella Artois, 1 piece of summer sausage
7:20 p.m.: 1 morphine, 9:30 p.m.: 1
  morphine

It was Saturday, Labor Day weekend. Chrissy and I had snuck out for a couple of hours the night before, leaving Peggy in charge. Yes, I was a tiny bit hungover; I might as well admit that right out of the chute. The birds outside my bedroom window woke me up way too early. They're pretty to look at, sure, but when they're just out there, behind the shades, making noise on a Saturday morning, not so much. I flipped onto my stomach, pulled a pillow over my head, and wishing I had a shotgun, tried to go back to sleep. It was no use, though, because my bladder was awake too.

The house was dark, except for a few slivers of morning sun peeping through the dining room windows. Coming out of the bathroom, I looked down the hall and saw my father asleep. He looked peaceful and small. Cancer had taken weight off him so his CPAP machine had gone into the closet. Suddenly, like a little kid, I was overcome with the urge to climb in bed with him one more time. I wanted to grab a moment, one that was only his and mine, a quiet memory I could hang on to when all was said and done.

So I crawled in the bed, curled up next to him, and watched the pink wool blanket rise and fall along with his breathing. The ceiling fan whispered a little breeze over the two of us. I didn't think anything, at least not that I can remember. I wanted to have deep thoughts. I really did. I wanted the journey, our friendship, everything, to come into focus. I wanted to be struck by a profound insight, some untapped philosophy about life and death, fathers and daughters. But George was dying; what else was there to know? I didn't think. Instead, I lay my head on the pillow and put my hand on his shoulder. There was something harmonious about his breathing. His inhale and exhale were tempered and patient, like the birth of a new day. It was a tender moment indeed, chock-full of dramatic effect—as in, cue the theme song from *Terms of Endearment*. I knew it even then, and I was happy. But here's the thing about tender moments . . . um . . . they're tender, delicate, vulnerable to even the slightest variation in circumstance.

I closed my eyes, and before I knew what was happening the tiniest burp slipped out of my mouth. Honestly, it was infinitesimal, nothing more than a wee little hiccup, really.

"Julia?" he said, not moving.

"Yeah, Dad," I said, anticipating something heartfelt and emotional.

"What did you eat for dinner last night?"

I rolled over and looked up at the ceiling fan. I tried to focus on just one blade as it whipped around in circles, but the motion made my eyeballs throb. "Um . . . let's see . . . chicken enchiladas and about ninety-five beers."

"Ugh." He reached for the stainless-steel bowl—the same stainless-steel bowl my mother had peed in, the same bowl we continued to use to mix cookie dough and cucumber salad.

"Why?"

"Your *breath* is *gagging* me."

"Well," I said, chuckling, "I've got some really bad news for you, then."

"What?" he whimpered.

"I just farted." Again, infinitesimal, I swear. "And I think it might be a—"

Before I could finish my sentence, he barfed. And just like that, our tender moment vanished.

I wish I could say I helped him, but I didn't. Instead, I cracked up laughing, rolled off the bed, and staggered down the hall. Shameful, sure. Embarrassing, absolutely. What else can I say? The truth is . . . sometimes reality stinks.

Antinausea, 1 morphine
Stella
1 morphine

Labor Day was different. It brought the grandchildren and a much sweeter reality, thank God. We had just finished dinner. I sat outside on the patio with a couple of the kids, poking my way around a battered pile of beef stew. George wasn't a griller. He said it was too much of a hassle. So we didn't do traditional Labor Day food—hamburgers, bratwursts, hot dogs, and chips on flimsy paper plates—like normal people. No, we did beef stew on my mother's Wedgwood. The beef had been found in the back of the freezer, marked "St. Robert's Tips, 2005."

As I set my plate aside, one of my nephews, Michael, asked, "Can I borrow this book?"

"I think you can have it. Go ask Grandpa." As I watched the screen door slam behind him, I thought, *These kids really know him. They knew her too.*

My parents were themselves as grandparents. They didn't know how to be anything else. There was nothing multigenerational about their behavior. They were not touchy-feely; they did not have cute grandparent nicknames like Nana or Papa. They did not get down on the floor and play with my nieces and nephews, and they sure as hell did not babysit. The grandkids began piling up when I was just seven years old, long before my parents were ready, and one after another they marched into life until the number finally plateaued at twenty-four. My parents' footing was precarious, I think, because their timing was off. The gap between their babies and their babies' babies simply wasn't wide enough. Still, they found ways to connect. My mother bought the gifts: birthdays, baptisms, First Holy Communions, confirmations, graduations, and Christmases. During Lent, when she quit smoking, she knit them sweaters, hats, and mittens, and the rest of the year she bought fancy Florence Eiseman stuff. Terry didn't do trendy and she didn't do cheap. She didn't shop, either. Are you kidding? Shopping was for people with one, two, or even fifteen gifts to purchase. No, Terry didn't shop, she bought. The people at Louise Godell, a children's clothing shop on Silver Spring, scurried around frantically, licking their chops, when they saw her plugging dimes in the parking meter.

She was casually conversational with the grandkids, the same way she was with us, coffee in one hand and cigarette in the other. She was easy, approachable, and didn't beat around the bush. Her map of the teenage psyche was tattered and worn, sure, but it didn't matter; she was a pro at picking her way in the dark. Plus, she'd been over it a thousand times. Terry found her way in with them because she knew how to follow the crumbs. She knew which crumbs to pick up—faith and friendship, prudence and modesty—and knew which ones to leave behind—long hair, multiple piercings, loud music, mumbling, and sullenness.

And every year in July, George took them places, the girls and the boys separately. They went to the American Players Theatre and the House on the Rock in Spring Green, the National Mustard Museum in Mount Horeb, the Wisconsin Maritime Museum in Manitowoc, the top of the John Hancock Center in Chicago, and the Mark Twain Boyhood Home and Museum in Hannibal, Missouri. In time, these little excursions became affectionately known as the Grandpa Trips.

There were rules. Rule number one: no parents were allowed. Rule number two: you had to be eight years old in order to go on the Grandpa Trips. This rule was broken only once. Julia, my sister Amy's daughter and the youngest grandchild, was literally grandfathered in at age five. George never gave a reason. He didn't need to. It was his trip. Rule number three: the older kids were "in charge" of the younger ones. Rule number four, instituted later, when the older kids could drive: no speeding.

Walkin'-around money was handed out. At the beginning of each trip, while sitting at a restaurant of George's choosing (one that had a bar), they all received twice their age in crisp new bills, folded neatly in embroidered coin purses. With this money, the kids were allowed to buy whatever crap they wanted—stickers, beads, fireworks, or plastic dinosaurs. Of course, they had an elaborate system of fines too. If someone asked, "How long until we get there?" he or she was fined a quarter. The kids were allowed to order anything they wanted for lunch or dinner, but if they didn't finish their meal, they had to pull out their walkin'-around money and pay for it themselves. As far as I know, it happened only once, and then the brokering arose. Meals were shared. The persnickety and the nondiscriminating eaters negotiated their way through pancakes, French fries, and steaks, and waste was eliminated.

After Terry and George moved back to Milwaukee, the Grandpa Trips ended on that patio. My siblings, the ones who had kids on the trip, would come over, sit around, and wait for the cars to pull up. It was always a whirlwind of stories about the plays, sure, or the museum, yes, but there were other stories too—about thirteen girls dancing in a downpour, which kid fell in a lake, which kid slept on the radiator, and which kid ordered a forty-dollar steak.

This Labor Day was quieter. I picked up my plate, went back into the house, and saw small stacks of books sitting on the kitchen counter, in the window bay, and on the couch. The other grandkids had followed Michael's lead, picking out books. They chose poetry, religion, philosophy, and sports, whatever interested them, whatever they deemed inherently Grandpa. George did not buy books willy-nilly. The books he chose were always tied to an event in his life. Each one had a story bigger than its pages. Newspaper articles, theater tickets, and scribbled notes slipped to the floor as the kids stood around and leafed through the pages of Shakespeare, Dante, and Joyce. One by one they picked them up, carried them back to Grandpa's room, and asked him to share the reason behind the purchase.

Leaning back on a dining room chair, I caught glimpses of them. Maggie, Chrissy's daughter—twelve and lanky, with perfect skin, a tangled mess of blond hair, and a mouth full of braces—kneeling in bed next to my father, giggling, at what I didn't know. And Julia, who was just six, sitting on a stool next to George, trying to read her choice to him. The story was about Valentine's Day, a spin-off of *The Night before Christmas*. George held one side of the book in his hand and she held the other in hers. He let her stumble through the first few pages before scooping her into the bed beside him. She laid her head on the pillow and stuck her thumb in her mouth, and he took over the reading. I noticed he kept his eyes open.

9/14, 6:30 a.m.: Antinausea gel
11:00 a.m.: Morphine
2:30 p.m.: Nausea gel

4:00 p.m.: Morphine
Vomiting
6:30 p.m.: Antinausea gel
1 raspberry, Stella
8:00 p.m.: Morphine, patch change

Like it or not, death comes with accoutrements. Necessity carries them across the threshold, and before you know it, you're making room for the adjustable bed, the tray table, the emesis basin, the mouth swabs, the A+D ointment, and the baby monitor. The night before Terry died I remember my father looking around at all the hospice equipment and saying very matter-of-factly, "It's hard work being born, and it's hard work dying." A bit of an understatement, sure, but so true. If you're lucky enough to prepare, on either side, the beginning and the end are both crowded with a slew of very similar accessories, designed for the most part around convenience, comfort, and safety. Glaring as it is, the circumstances provide the only real difference.

So necessity did its thing, and we did ours, and George trusted. Trust. That was the key. It allowed us to exist in the bizarre three-part palliative harmony. New things found their way in and either kicked out or demanded space among the old. I remember lying in his hospital bed one night, looking around, waiting while

Chrissy helped him in the bathroom. I heard the two of them talking, but their words sounded like drizzle, indistinct, muffled. It was not the original bedroom, of course—the rose-print wallpaper, brittle and peeling along the base-boards, the speckled green carpeting, and the dusty blinds were all different—but it was undeniably my parents' bedroom. There was the bust of Jesus, standing on George's dresser; the Madonna and Child sitting on Terry's lingerie chest; and St. Thérèse of Lisieux hanging on the wall next to the door, above the light switch. These folks had been there since the beginning. These folks my mother carried across the threshold.

St. Thérèse stared at me. The picture had peripheral vision, which I suppose would have been terrific if she were an actual person standing in the room. But she was flat, inanimate, and anchored in a frame, so her wandering eyes were scary. My spine tingled. I casually shifted my gaze somewhere, anywhere else, hoping she wouldn't notice. In the chair next to the bed, within arm's reach, sat the stainless-steel barf bowl, a damp washcloth slung over its side. The newspaper was folded and perched on a pile of books someone had stacked on the floor. And on his nightstand were morphine packets, fanned out—four of a kind—a tube of antinausea gel, a box of latex gloves, a

271

borrowed baby monitor, a half glass of Stella, and George's broken rosary.

He never actually said the rosary, at least not that I ever saw. He just thumbed the dark wooden beads in his pocket. I think they provided comfort. The chain's link was broken right where the mysteries began. Joyful, Luminous, Sorrowful, Glorious; different depending on the day and the season. And the crucifix was lost. Still, it had been a gift from my mother and he carried it everywhere. I watched him place it in a hundred plastic airport security bins over the years— Milwaukee, Chicago, London, Newark, Rome, and Dublin.

George clung to the notion that he would pass away quietly in his sleep. Really, who could blame him? "I think tonight's the night, girls," he said again, and Chrissy and I both laughed.

"Here, Dad," she said, handing him the rosary.

He slipped it slowly from one palm to the other and stared at it pensively, rolling the soft wood between his fingers. I couldn't say what he was thinking. I didn't ask. It occurred to me, though, for just a second, that his greatest mystery, *the* greatest mystery, was about to be explained. Finally, he wrapped his fist around a handful of beads and held them up.

"I want you girls to know," he said, letting a couple of strands slip through his fingers, "just because I have this with me doesn't mean I'm actually saying it."

Honestly.

"Okay, Dad," I said.

"I don't want anyone thinking I've become ultrareligious all of a sudden."

Chrissy rolled her eyes. "I wouldn't worry about it, Dad."

"Yeah, Dad," I said, "if someone from Opus Dei calls—"

"Tell 'em I'm in a coma."

"You got it," I said, laughing.

Twenty minutes later, Chrissy and I were cleaning up the kitchen when we heard him stir. "Shhh," Chrissy said, turning off the tap and leaning into the receiver of the baby monitor. "Listen."

A dry towel in one hand and a dripping pot in the other, I tiptoed next to her, as if he could hear me.

"Take and receive, O Lord, all my liberty, all my memory, all my understanding . . ."

"What is that?" I asked.

"Shhh," she repeated, and held up her hand. "It's the—"

"You have given me all that I am . . ."

"—St. Ignatius prayer."

"All that I possess; I surrender it all to you that you may dispose of it according to your will . . ."

A massive lump formed in my throat and took

my breath away. I held my fist over my mouth, looked over at Chrissy, and saw a painfully bittersweet expression staring back at me.

Antinausea
Morphine
Vomiting
Antinausea
Apple sauce
Prune juice
Stella

I expected Father Tim. I had called him in the morning on my way to work and asked if he would come over and see George. It's what Catholics do. We call the priest. We get blessings. We cover our bases. George had been in and out of lucidity for days, so we figured it was time. But when I walked into his room, I found my dad's doctor, Ted O'Reilly, sitting in the chair next to the bed.

"Hi, Dr. O'Reilly."

"Hi."

"What brings you over?" He was George's general practitioner. He had been off the case for months, but we called him now and then to pick his brain.

"I just wanted to check in and see how things were going with my friend here."

He put his hand on George's shoulder. My

father liked Dr. O'Reilly; we all did. He was a cutie-pie—auburn hair, round apple cheeks, blue eyes, kind smile, nice bod, the whole package. Plus, he helped Terry die, and he did it well. No extraordinary measures; he just sat on the edge of her bed, took her hand, and told her it was time. Believe me, it's not something you see every day. Doctors do life, not death.

"I picked up a six-pack of Stella on my way home. You want one?"

He hesitated for a second, and then said, "Yeah, sure, why not, I'm not on call."

Katie, Peggy, and Amy were drifting about the house. Eventually we all ended up sitting around George's bed, chatting, each of us with a small glass of beer. Headlights shined on the wall and a car door slammed.

Father Tim let himself in. "What's this?" he said, laughing as he made his way down the hall. "I thought I was coming to give you last rites and you're sitting here drinking a beer."

George giggled and twitched.

"Do you want one, Father Tim?" Katie asked.

"No . . . I'm sorry, I can't. I've got a thing—"

"C'mon, it's Stella," she prodded.

He shook his head, about to decline again, and then he paused. I saw the look in his eye change. He had expected sadness and foreboding; instead, he found an accidental party. I knew he would stay. There was a homily in it.

275

"Sure, what the heck."

I poured him a glass and handed it to him.

"This is made in Belgium, you know, in Leuven. I studied there."

"Kate! Kate!" George burst in. "Go get that *Manneken Pis* off the mantel."

Katie, Peggy, Amy, and I exchanged apprehensive looks. We were all thinking the same thing. *He's talking like a sausage.* It was a Terry expression. An equivalent idiom today might be, WTF?

"What was that, Dad? German?" I asked.

"No. Kate, go get it," he demanded. "It's on the mantel."

"Okay," Katie said doubtfully, leaving the room.

"What're you talking about, Dad?" Amy asked.

"The *Manneken Pis*. It's a statue—"

"I know what he's talking about," Father Tim said. "It's a statue in Leuven, of a boy—"

"Yes, yes!" George exclaimed, raising his glass. "It's a statue of a boy pissing."

Father Tim smiled. "He's right."

"Here, bring it here," George said, waving Katie back into the room.

We all leaned forward and followed her hand. Sure enough, he was right. It was a three-and-a-half-inch bronze likeness of a boy pissing.

"Where did you get that, Dad?" Amy laughed.

"I brought it home from the war."

"Where has it been?"

"On the mantel!" said the sausage, as if my sisters and I had all been born blind. I had never seen it before in my life, but I wasn't about to argue. Besides, I knew my mother well enough to figure out that there was no way she'd have let a statue like that hang around a house with nine kids. She had a hard enough time keeping a lid on the potty-talk. The last thing she needed was a little naked wiener, bronze or not, hanging out—pardon the pun—on the mantel. I assumed George had discovered it in a box after she died.

"Tell the story, George," Father Tim said, gesturing with his glass.

So he did. George told the story with a clarity we hadn't seen in a while, a story about a little boy, the son of a wealthy merchant, who had gone missing in Leuven. The merchant formed a search party and made the promise that if his beloved son was found, wherever he was found, whatever he was doing, he would build a statue in grateful thanksgiving to God. The boy, it turned out, was found, taking a leak.

We looked to Father Tim for verification, and he nodded. That was the story.

The conversation continued. We talked about nothing in particular, just cocktail party gibber-jabber. The toilet in the bathroom was on the fritz and had been running for days. Whoever moved George's king-size bed out to the garage had carelessly dropped the box spring on my front bike tire. Father Tim and Dr. O'Reilly agreed to help us move it. Brett Favre had broken Dan Marino's touchdown record. The weather was changing. The days had grown shorter.

Father Tim's blessing came on the heels of a toast to family, friends, and George. The seven of us clasped hands, said an Our Father, and received Holy Communion. George closed his eyes and folded his hands and we left him alone. Sure, he had a few hang-ups where the church was concerned; he feigned disbelief and called it hocus-pocus, but he cherished the presence of the Risen Lord in Holy Communion. Transubstantiation, it's a mind-bender for most Catholics. This one, George took on faith.

Later, when we tucked him in and said our good nights and our "just in case" good-byes, he said, "Now *that* was an Academy Award–winning night."

10/20, 2:00 a.m.: 2 morphine, 2 anti-nausea
7:30 a.m.: 2 morphine, 2 antinausea, 1 dropper

My father died that afternoon. In the end it was simple and quiet. A bunch of us were there—Amy, Jimmy, Ashley, Katie, Peggy, and me—crowded around his bed, watching his chest sporadically rise and fall. In his lap we laid his broken rosary, a picture of our mother, and a red rose. We touched him. We prayed, and we whispered, "It's okay, Dad. It's okay." Stevie arrived around one thirty, sat down, and gently slipped George's hand inside his own. I sat there, across from my brother, letting silent tears drop into pink blankets and staring at those hands, folded together. It was a gift, that moment, one full grace that only the beginning and the end can offer. My father's hand was fragile, worn, and ragged; Stevie's was smooth and strong. The two were bound together, yet separated by a generation and a breath, holding on and letting go.

Naturally, a party ensued. I know, I know, but let's face it, grief can get a little boring. So one by one, we trickled out to the patio, while family, friends, and neighbors trickled up the driveway. It was a gorgeous October day, high sixties and sunny. The kind of day George would have loved. Wisconsin weather will do that, serve up something beautiful and warm right in the middle of bitter and cold. We made drinks and funeral arrangements and we celebrated George's life into the evening.

The party was still going strong when I called it a night. I walked down the hallway and into my father's room. His body was gone, zipped into a nonporous black bag and carted down Lake Drive in the back of a minivan. The plastic hospital bed mattress crunched as I sat on its edge. Chatter and music drifted through the windows, along with the scent of a fall fire from the pit on the patio. A log popped. Someone had dusted George's nightstand, stacked his books in a neat little pile, largest to smallest, and swept the hospice debris into the garbage can on the floor. His rosary and his watch were left sitting next to the lamp. I picked up the watch and stretched the silver band with my fingers. It was a woman's watch, though not particularly feminine. George had brought it back from Switzerland after the war, a gift for his mother. Presumably he took it back when she died. He wore it all the time. I slid it around my wrist, grabbed the broken rosary in my fist, kissed it, and went to bed.

THE NEXT MORNING I woke up on top of my bedspread, wearing what I had on the night before, with the rosary still in my grip. The house was quiet and dark. I wondered if I was alone. After all, there was no longer a need for two of us to be in the house. I got up, found Katie asleep in the guest room, and saw that someone had closed George's bedroom door. I remember making for the knob and thinking, *I can't have that.* Death had done something to the air. Overnight, it had become thick. Dragging my body down the hallway was like footslogging through a vat of

Jell-O. I opened my father's bedroom door and let the morning breeze flow through the house.

It was another sunny day, though cooler. I walked outside to get the paper. The screen door clapped against its frame as my stocking feet hit the chilly patio bricks.

"Good morning," a voice called from across the street.

I looked up and saw our neighbor and old friend of my parents, Mrs. Hoff. She had been over the night before, toasting George.

"Morning," I smiled, and tiptoed toward her. We embraced around the basket she carried in the crook of her arm. It felt good to hug someone's parent.

"This is for you kids," she said, holding out the basket. Something about her reminded me of Terry—her expression, maybe her red lipstick.

"Ah," I said, sighing, taking the basket and looking over the goods. It was overflowing with a dozen eggs, bacon, sausage, bread, fresh-squeezed orange juice, and coffee. "Brunch comes to us today. Thank you. Thank you. Thank you."

THE OBITUARY READ: "Pandl owned acclaimed Bayside restaurant." I coasted my car to a stop at the corner of Lake Drive and Brown Deer Road and looked over at the building. Inside, brunch preparations were being made. Through the windows, I saw waitstaff shifting and setting tables. Billy, the dishwasher, was picking up the parking lot. The world was still spinning. Wind kicked dry leaves across the road as I headed south, and sunlight danced around brown, red, and gold. I felt oddly disconnected, like I didn't belong, like a party crasher. Something was missing. George, of course, but there was something else too. I rolled down the window, held my arm out, and let the breeze sweep through my fingers. Then it dawned on me: the daughter. She was gone too. She had drawn her last breath and disappeared into the past along with her father. I was somebody else.

Walking into St. Hedwig's, I dunked my finger in the holy water font and blessed myself, *in the name of the Father, the Son, and the Holy Spirit, Amen.* I took my place in a pew toward the back and closed my eyes.

"I'll be here." That's what my father had said to me when we finally did get our tender moment. I was sitting on his bed, holding his hand and trying to keep a stiff upper lip. The only words I could summon were, "I'm sure gonna miss you, Dad." He tightened his grip, gave my hand a little tug, smiled, and said, "I'll be here. I'll be here."

That was it. Simple.

Three little words.

Three and a half, really.

He was right.

Acknowledgments

To Dan Lazar, a million and one thanks for finding this book, for loving it, and for holding my hand throughout this whole process. To Chuck Adams and the entire team at Algonquin, thank you for believing in me, and George, for giving our story an opportunity to flourish and for having faith in a beginner.

Many thanks to Daniel Goldin and Lanora Haradon for giving this book two wonderful places to call home from the start.

To Bill Boelter, many thanks for keeping me employed, and to the gang at the Boelter SuperStore, thanks for being so flexible. To my family and friends around Wisconsin and the country, Chrissy & Bill, Pam & Tom, Patty & Mike, Patty, Clare, Kathy, Nikki, Shannon, Betsy, Peggy, Anne, Jenna & Margaret, thank you for booking events and spreading the word. And to those of you whom I will be hitting up in the near future, thank you in advance. To every book club that has invited me to join them so far, thank you for the delicious food, drinks, and conversation.

To Debbie, Debbie, and Jayson, my beloved San Jamar friends, thanks for being so understanding when I quit what was, without a doubt, the best job I'll ever have. Thanks for reading my pages month after month, typos and all. And thanks for not letting me run up those bar tabs alone. Todd, thanks for taking the glamour shot. I don't do glamour, so I know it wasn't easy. Peggy, Gerry, Meg, Lisa, Susie, Julie B., Shelly, Cris, Patti, and Craig, thanks for listening to me prattle on about writing this book for the past twenty years and for encouraging me to finally take the leap and do it. Paul Burgoyne, thanks for helping me step on to the right path. Tom Pop, thanks for teaching me how to fold pizza. Maddy Steele, thanks for choosing a piece of the book for competition and taking it out for a test drive. Judy, even though it made me want to cry, thanks for advising me to retype. Carolyn, thanks so much for your first words of encouragement. You have no idea how they helped me keep going. Thanks for your fabulous editing and your honest commentary. I never would have finished without you.

If I have forgotten you, come on over and I'll make you dinner.

Afterword

Shortly before the completion of this book, on Sunday, November 15, 2009, Pandl's in Bayside was closed. The last meal served was indeed a brunch. The 8825 North Lake Drive location is now home to a synagogue. The celebration continues.

Shalom.

Center Point Large Print

600 Brooks Road / PO Box 1
Thorndike ME 04986-0001 USA

(207) 568-3717

US & Canada:
1 800 929-9108
www.centerpointlargeprint.com